S0-BYB-537

Making Sense of
Social Theory

Making Sense of Social Theory

A Practical Introduction

Charles H. Powers

ROWMAN & LITTLEFIELD PUBLISHERS, INC.
Lanham • Boulder • New York • Toronto • Oxford

ROWMAN & LITTLEFIELD PUBLISHERS, INC.

Published in the United States of America
by Rowman & Littlefield Publishers, Inc.
A wholly owned subsidiary of The Rowman & Littlefield Publishing Group, Inc.
4501 Forbes Boulevard, Suite 200, Lanham, MD 20706
www.rowmanlittlefield.com

P.O. Box 317, Oxford OX2 9RU, UK

Copyright © 2004 by Rowman & Littlefield Publishers, Inc.

All rights reserved. No part of this publication may
be reproduced, stored in a retrieval system, or transmitted
in any form or by any means, electronic, mechanical,
photocopying, recording, or otherwise, without the prior
permission of the publisher.

British Library Cataloguing in Publication Information Available

Library of Congress Cataloging-in-Publication Data

Powers, Charles H.
   Making sense of social theory : a practical introduction / Charles H.
Powers.
      p.   cm.
Includes bibliographical references and index.
   ISBN 0-7425-3046-9 (alk. paper) — ISBN 0-7425-3047-7 (pbk. : alk.
paper)
   1. Sociology—History.   2. Sociology—Philosophy.   3. Schools of
sociology.   I. Title.
   HM435 .P69   2004
   301'.01—dc22   2003020934

Printed in the United States of America

∞ ™ The paper used in this publication meets the minimum requirements of
American National Standard for Information Sciences—Permanence of Paper for
Printed Library Materials, ANSI/NISO Z39.48–1992.

To Catlin and Bonnie, who continue to give me as much love and understanding as a father could hope for

Contents

Preface

Making Sense of Social Theory is written for students. By design, it is short, clear, and manageable. For that reason, using this book should raise the level of discourse among students receiving their first concentrated exposure to sociological theory. The text will elevate student interest in and mastery over material many tend to assume will be arcane and boring. Use of this book will enhance students' awareness of themselves as social science professionals, having something to offer specifically because (not in spite of) the fact that they majored in sociology.

The text is divided into four parts. Part I consists of chapters explaining the role of theory in a science like sociology. Part II introduces some of the most enduring social science insights pioneered by the principal founders of sociology. Part III introduces some of the influential lines of theoretical analysis that developed once sociology gained momentum in the middle of the twentieth century. And part IV recaps sociological insights that can be practically applied by readers.

Most introductory theory books try to be encyclopedic, reviewing a great deal of literature and covering many of the nuances in that literature. This one is different, and intentionally so. A valuable feature of it is that it consolidates many of the most fundamental insights of sociology into a coherent package, while conveying to students what it means to be a social *scientist*, and providing a basic introduction to theory for sociology as a social *science* discipline. The aim is to help students become better sociologists (a) by acquiring a very basic and sound conceptual and historical map of the discipline; (b) by more consciously focusing on, and more deeply internalizing, a few of sociology's most powerful explanatory principles; and (c) by cultivating a deeper and more realistic appreciation for sociology's promise as a science.

This book is written with a different sense of mission than standard *surveys* of sociological theory. Standard survey textbooks, by definition and design, try to maximize range of coverage. In contrast, this book is written as a very *basic* introduction. It is rudimentary. It highlights only the most fundamental points, expressing those points as clearly as possible to facilitate practical learning and application. Readers will finish this book with a reasonably well-integrated and coherent sense of sociological theory as a whole. Readers will then be better equipped to understand and appreciate other theoretical works they might encounter. In following this approach, I have written down information from three decades of trial and error in teaching theory, and three decades of contact with alums discussing what theory content they found of most value in their lives after graduation. I want students to transition out of college, armed as much as possible with the analytical and explanatory power of sociology at their disposal. This book is written with that goal in mind, keeping things simple by focusing exclusively on what is most important, so that readers acquire a skeletal framework with its most obvious features in plain view, unobscured by much detail.

Acknowledgments

I am indebted to the many sociological theorists I have had the benefit of interacting with over the years. Chief among them are Jonathan Turner, Jerald Hage, Robert Dubin, Ralph Turner, Randall Collins, Harry Johnson, and Harold Garfinkel. Another kind of intellectual debt is owed to people who have helped me work out the themes and issues covered in this book. In this regard, I am indebted to many people, including Joan Powers, Marilyn Fernandez, Ray Maghroori, Andrew Sofranko, Karen McGovern, Donald Powers, Laura Nichols, Witold Krassowski, Demetra Kalogrides, Suzanne Szabo, Susan Rigdon, Nancy Brennan, Jürgen Backhaus, Gerrit Meijer, Mitch Allen, Bill Hunter, Everlee Jones, Edward O'Boyle, Richard Moodey, and William Corsaro, to name a just a few. My special thanks also go to the people at Rowman & Littlefield who made the production of this book possible: Dave Compton, Alla Corey, Jessica Gribble, April Leo, Susan McEachern, and Alan McClare. And of pivotal importance, special acknowledgment goes to Stephen McNamee for penetrating reviewer comments that led to many improvements in manuscript. Since I have had the good fortune of support and encouragement from very talented people, the faults remaining in this manuscript are solely my responsibility.

Part I

Understanding What Theory Is About

Part I offers an intellectual framework for understanding sociology as a social science. For that reason, part I should help readers better appreciate the full importance of content presented in the remainder of the book. Understanding part I is crucial for achieving the learning objectives this book is designed to foster. Sometimes, readers glance over introductory chapters, thinking that the difficult material and core material will come later. That isn't the case with this book. The first chapter contains more conceptually difficult nuances than any other chapter in the book, and the three chapters of part I alert readers about the kinds of things to look for when reading the rest of the book. Time spent trying to really understand the first three chapters will be time well spent.

Part II and part III cover standard theory content. Part II introduces some of the giants of sociological theory, focusing on the works of Emile Durkheim, Karl Marx, Max Weber, and George Herbert Mead and also introducing readers to sociology's intellectual roots in the discipline of economics and to sociology's initiative of urban ethnography as an avenue of study. Part III offers readers a conceptual grasp of four theoretical frameworks that developed in sociology: structural–functionalism, conflict theory, symbolic interaction, and exchange theory. One will find this list of people and perspectives (or at least very similar lists) in other books on sociological theory. But the approach used in this book is quite different from approaches found in other books. This book (a) explicitly and self-consciously employs a science approach, identifying predictive insights and exploring how these insights can be used to understand real

1

world events better, and (b) continually strives to focus attention on those most widely used theoretical insights from sociology that are reasonably simple (unambiguous in meaning), highly robust (apply in different situations), and very powerful (explain big differences and not just small ones).

Perhaps more than any other book available, this one adopts a self-conscious, consistent, and workable (practical, nonpolemic) science approach. The books that come closest, such as Jonathan H. Turner's excellent work *The Structure of Sociological Theory*, are different in their concern for detail. More detailed books place high value (perhaps highest value) on the thoroughness of their coverage of theory content. The less detail-oriented strategy followed in this book places a very high value on conveying a basic understanding of what social science really means and what the fundamental connection between theory and research must be when sociology is practiced as a science.[1] A lot of people have difficulty making a connection between theory and research. This book clarifies what that connection is, and in the process makes it easier to make the connection.

One of my goals is to invite readers to really use theory while experiencing what may be their first systematic exposure to sociological theory as a subject. In this respect, the prepublication versions of this book that I developed for use in my own classes were quite successful. This success is achieved by limiting detail and focusing on a few immensely important predictive insights that have applicability in a wide range of settings.

This book employs a proven pedagogy. Over the years, I have used pretests and posttests while experimenting with teaching/learning strategies. The challenge has been to facilitate learning on the part of students who, by and large, would prefer not to have to take a theory course. At first, the results of my pre- and posttests were disheartening. When I first began using pretests and posttests, it seemed that students came into my theory classes less familiar with sociological theory than I had assumed they would be and left my class less comfortable with theory material than I expected them to be. My challenge as a teacher was to do something about this. Over a period of years, I worked to perfect a method for helping students understand more theory and apply that theory material more consistently in conjunction with what they encounter elsewhere. What I have learned is that my students grasp theory better and apply it more once exposed to the science vision communicated in this book. Using this approach, my students learn more, learn faster, have more fun, are more likely to feel intellectually alive, are more interested in theory when they engage in research, are more apt to design research in order to learn something rather than validate what they already believe, invoke theory more often at jobs and in their internships, present themselves better in job interviews, and enjoy better career trajectories. But all this takes work on the part of students and direction supplied by faculty.

In 1998, the undergraduate program I teach in received the American Sociological Association's Distinguished Contributions to Teaching Award for curricular innovations. Those innovations have largely revolved around the active and successful intertwining of theory with the rest of the sociology curriculum. This book is a by-product of that effort.

In my experience, the keys to teaching/learning success are (a) reducing material to manageable bits most sociologists agree on, (b) delivering material in the clearest possible way in order to reduce fear and frustration, and (c) devoting some time to application so that students can see the relevance of material for real life. This approach to teaching involves *focusing on what is most important* rather than smothering students with more detail than they are willing to digest on first contact. And it requires asking students to *apply ideas to the real world as they experience it*. This book is written with those lessons of pedagogy in mind. The teaching method used here stresses clarity, repetition, and application, and has worked well.

NOTE

1. Jonathan Turner, *The Structure of Sociological Theory*, 7th ed. (Belmont, Calif.: Wadsworth, 2002).

1

EMBRACING THE SUBJECT

Becoming a Better Social Scientist by Learning More about Sociological Theory

A PERSONAL NOTE TO STUDENTS

I would like to begin on a personal note to those readers who happen to be students taking their first sociological theory course. Over time, my students have taught me two important lessons about teaching theory. The first lesson is that learning theory is work. Students have to read and think about the material and apply the material in order for the course to be successful. No one can do those things for you except yourself. The second lesson I have learned is this: if there is too much material or if the material is too confusing, many students will shut down before they really give themselves a chance to master the subject. This is a tragedy any time, but especially in a sociological theory course. Learning theory is a necessary step in developing an accurate and coherent understanding of the discipline. With that in mind, this book is written as a first exposure to theory. It is short and clear. There is no reason this book should turn off any student who has a reasonable degree of commitment to study. Carefully reading this text should be well worth the investment of time and effort for anyone wanting a coherent introduction to the role of theory in the discipline of sociology.

This book codifies insights sociologists keep returning to because of their explanatory power. By codifying some of the key ideas sociologists continue to adhere to, this book provides readers with a theory tool kit. The integrative science-based view this book encourages, and the explanatory tool kit it provides, make the book worth treating seriously and keeping for future reference. Although I do not attempt to cover everything one finds in more encyclopedic theory books, I do invite those new to sociology to stand on common ground with established sociologists by recognizing and pondering questions of central theoretical significance. The text focuses on those insights sociologists are most confident about, and those insights that are most easily applied in a wide range of real settings and situations; it covers material that may be especially useful in jobs and life, precisely because it stays centered on the most robust and enduring of our sociological insights.

This first chapter is the hardest, because it contains the greatest number of nuances (fine distinctions that turn out later to be important). People who get off to a strong start by reading the first chapter carefully and thinking about its meaning will have an easier time later on.

SOCIOLOGY AS A SCIENCE

Sociology is considered a social science. Being a *science* means that there is a *commitment to using observations of the real world over time in trying to develop explanations that are even better than the ones we already have.* A body of work that fails to use evidence about the real world in order to develop and test explanatory frameworks may indeed be interesting. It may be important. It may be worthwhile. But it is not "science" in any accurate sense of the term.

The data social scientists use can be "quantitative." That is, it can be easily translatable into numbers signifying magnitude or the degree to which different cases possess a set of traits on which those cases are compared. Or data can be "qualitative," allowing for a contrast of differences in fundamental form between cases. Whether quantitative or qualitative, it is important to remember how data about the real world are used. A scientist does not set out to manipulate data to "prove" her or his theories to be correct. A scientist uses data to triangulate on ways that our theories seem inaccurate or incomplete, for the entire idea behind science is to make progress by improving our theories over time. Far from assuming existing knowledge claims of accuracy, science presumes that existing knowledge claims are all provisional. Scientists realize that what they know is not really "truth" as such. It is merely the closest formulation we are presently able to devise to explain what we can observe about the world around us.

To the extent that an academic discipline such as sociology is practiced as a real science, *theory occupies a special place* for three important reasons. First, theory is what scientists (social scientists or any other kind of scientists) use to convey what we currently think we "know" about the way the world works. In other words, theory captures our best present understanding. It emphasizes what we think we know that extends *beyond the realm of whatever was widely understood as "common sense"* before the discipline came into existence. In this respect, theory consists of the real insight a discipline has to offer. Second, good theory identifies those questions that are most important for people in the discipline to try to answer next. And third, improvement in theory over time is the primary way progress is judged in a science. For, when theory is changing, we know that people are moving away from old modes of understanding toward new ones. That movement is "scientific" if it is governed by careful and theoretically informed hypothesis testing.

Science does move forward. In geology, for instance, plate tectonics was considered childish thinking until the early 1960s. Now our understanding has changed. This is an illustration of what we mean by scientific progress.

Most people now take plate tectonics for granted, as if this understanding of geology has always been obvious. But it was anything but obvious until a few decades ago. The very thought that entire continents might be sliding around, something like blocks of ice on a smooth surface, was thought of as quite ludicrous, even rationally unthinkable, until cumulative research produced a preponderance of evidence to support the theory. Now people take plate tectonics for granted. Similarly, a lot of people take sociological discoveries for granted, as if those discoveries were of things that had always been known. The truth is that, before sociology, people thought almost everything about society and individual behavior was either God given or genetically determined. The only reason there are people who think sociology is little more than common sense is that many of sociology's great discoveries have proven so useful that they have gained widespread acceptance with the passage of time, and most people have forgotten where they came from. Consider the concept of "self-fulfilling prophecy." It sounds centuries old. Indeed, it sounds biblical. But sociologist Robert K. Merton is the person who coined the phrase and brought it into contemporary use.[1] Merton also initially developed the concepts of "role model" and "focus groups," and he was just one sociologist. Every time you recognize someone using the focus group, employing the concept of "role model," or falling victim to their own self-fulfilling prophecy, it is quite appropriate to take a moment to think "That came from sociology; sociology has given us a lot." Many other sociologists have made similarly important observations that have subsequently been absorbed into the framework of common knowledge. This knowledge was not so common before sociology came along.

WHAT DO SOCIOLOGY'S EXPLANATORY INSIGHTS COVER?

As with any field, sociological attention is riveted to certain kinds of phenomena. Sociology is distinctive in the attention it pays to what lies *between* people, to what *links* individuals with others in the social world. Sociology extends beyond the consideration of individuals in isolation. In focusing on the social world, sociologists most often focus on three qualitatively different kinds of linkage between people: (a) direct interpersonal attachments, (b) shared beliefs, and (c) systemic interconnections, including regulatory constraint.

As practitioners of a science, sociologists aim for good description of these things and then seek to explain variation between cases. We also want to know about the consequences of any differences that emerge and seek to understand how to promote constructive change. This suggests a definition for scientific sociology based on what we try to do. Scientific sociology can be characterized as effort to develop (1) more accurate descriptions, (2) more compelling awareness of causes, (3) more thorough understanding of consequences, and (4) more useful ways to bring about desired change in the nature of (a) direct interpersonal attachments, (b) shared beliefs, and (c) systemic patterns of interconnection, including regulator constraint.

Every science is based on commitment to theoretically grounded empirical research aimed at producing better descriptions of reality, more realistic explanations of variation between cases (or within cases over time), more revealing understanding of ramifications and consequences, and more useful ways to intervene in order to bring about desired change. But sociology is distinctive in its subject matter and conceptual approach. The focus is on what goes on between people (that is, on what is social) rather than on what goes on within people. This distinguishes sociology from psychology and counseling. And sociologists try to develop a whole picture of society, in contrast to economics and political science, both of which tend to approach their subject material in more tightly focused ways. For most sociologists, everything that is economic and political is considered relevant to the social world and too important to ignore. Economists, by contrast, are more likely to consider what is political and social as tangential to the subject matter of economics, and political scientists are more likely to regard what is social and economic as, at least to a degree, somewhat tangential to the subject matter of political science. Having the much more narrow focus of economics or somewhat more narrow focus of political science has the advantage of making conceptualization easier. But sociologists believe that their more encompassing conceptual approach ultimately leads to a fuller and more realistic understanding. In any case, it is certainly broader. Readers need to keep in mind the broad goals of sociology as a social science. Our social scientific goals are (a) more accurate description of sociological phenomena (patterns of interpersonal attachments, shared beliefs, and systemic interconnections, including regulatory constraints), (b) better explanation of variability in those patterns, (c) more accurate anticipation of consequences resulting from patterns that emerge, and (d) development of theoretical insights to guide policies and shape programs producing better outcomes.

SPECIFIC GOALS TO BE ACHIEVED WITH THIS BOOK

Theory goals have to be ambitious because theory drives science. Indeed, improving explanatory theory is the ultimate purpose of the scientific enterprise. And science, by its nature, sets the ambitious goal of developing more informative theory so that we can better understand, anticipate, and react to events.

This text imposes two important expectations on readers: acquiring a workable understanding of the nature of the scientific enterprise and acquiring a usable social science framework by practicing the application of a few of sociology's most robust and powerful theoretical insights. This book makes it as easy as possible to satisfy these expectations by staying focused on a manageable number of sociology's most important theory discoveries. After finishing this book, readers should be able to do five different things.

First, after reading this book, readers should be able to list several of sociology's most useful axioms. Axioms are *assumptions* people make when trying to understand the nature of the world on a conceptual level. Theorists often make axiomatic assumptions they know are overstated, but that help us see things we might otherwise miss. For example, it is simply not true that people always act out of self-interest. But if we assume self-interested behavior and look for it, we often see things that are important to know and easy to overlook. So even if an axiom is imperfect, the explicit statement of an axiomatic assumption can help us improve our conceptual understanding, subsequently revealing important new empirical discoveries and eventually leading to new theoretical developments. Part of developing a coherent understanding of sociological theory is learning to identify the most common axiomatic assumptions sociologists make and keeping them in mind because they are useful. The axiomatic assumptions various groups of theorists make constitute the "metatheoretical" content of sociology's prevailing interpretive perspectives.

Second, and ultimately most important, readers will complete this material knowing some of sociology's predictive principles. Theoretical principles are explanatory cause-and-effect statements articulated at the level of general concepts. Well-developed theoretical principles can be used to (a) understand why outcomes are alike in some cases and different in others, (b) generate research hypotheses we can use to test and refine our ideas, and (c) suggest policies and programs to improve outcomes. Predictive principles are what distinguish "theory" from "metatheory." Metatheory consists of assumptions but lacks predictive principles. Theory contains metatheoretical assumptions and adds predictive principles.

Third, this book provides readers with a skeletal outline of the history of the discipline of sociology. It does so by introducing some of the sociologists who have made seminal contributions to the development of the field and by briefly summarizing the essence of their most noteworthy contributions within the intellectual context of their times. A few of the important people discussed are Emile Durkheim, Max Weber, Karl Marx, Herbert Mead, Robert Park, Talcott Parsons, Robert Merton, Herbert Blumer, George Homans, and Richard Emerson. An awareness of some of sociology's main explanatory perspectives (structural–functionalism, conflict theory, symbolic interactionism, and exchange theory) will emerge from our review of the discipline's development.

Fourth, this text conveys an integrated sense of the discipline by recognizing that different groups of sociological theorists have made distinct contributions that complement each other far more often than they negate each other. Some people have the erroneous perception that accepting the validity of theoretical premises associated with one school of thought requires the wholesale rejection of all other theoretical approaches. This simply is not true. All theoretical perspectives have made a contribution. Recognizing this, and being able to draw inspiration from each perspective, strengthens us as sociologists and as social scientists.

Fifth, readers will finish this book with a sense of the direction sociology may be heading in the future. A possible road map of future intellectual activity and direction can be projected from a few of the big questions that excite sociological curiosity and interest. Some of these questions will be introduced within the context of our review of the discipline.

LEVELS OF ANALYSIS IN SOCIAL SCIENTIFIC INQUIRY

Sociology's intellectual frameworks offer insight into what are often referred to as micro, meso, and macro levels of analysis. *Micro* phenomena are those having to do with individual thought, decision making, and action. Micro analyses typically focus on direct interpersonal relations. *Meso*-level events deal with organizational phenomena. Meso analyses most commonly look at process and change within complex organizations, including businesses, schools, government agencies, and nonprofit charity groups. *Macro* phenomena concern things that sweep across society at large. Macro analyses generally look at relatively long-term social trends (including fads having some longevity) and at the development of systems of regulatory control (stock markets and law enforcement, for example).

DISTINGUISHING BETWEEN AXIOMS AND PRINCIPLES

Teachers of sociological theory are often somewhat disappointed when students completing a theory class are confused and look at the material as an arcane "ivory tower" subject. The fact is that sociologists know many things that are well worth knowing. A little memorization makes it easy to access and apply these insights. This book brings several of sociology's most useful axioms and principles to the surface. A device this book uses to focus readers on theoretical tenets that are worth learning is to distinguish between axioms and principles, and to highlight them as we go along. Axioms and principles make up much of our disciplinary tool kit, so becoming comfortable with them will make it easier to read this book and capitalize on the knowledge the book contains.

Studying disciplinary history provides a good avenue for learning theory, and in this book we will cover the most important highpoints in sociology's historical development. When describing each major historical turning point, this book arrives at a succinct statement of at least one axiom or principle. Learning these axioms and principles will be important, for part of theory has to be the step bringing our current theoretical understanding to the surface so that we can test it more thoroughly and use it more consistently. This is what it means for a discipline to be a science. Using a scientific approach requires that we try to articulate axioms and principles that help us better understand the world and thereby better prepare ourselves to deal with real circumstances.

All principles in every science are provisional. That is, they are the best we have for now. To practice real science is to appreciate that our current level of understanding will eventually be superseded by a more penetrating level of understanding. To do science is to utilize empirical observation in a process of theoretically informed hypothesis testing designed to take us to a higher (although never perfect or complete) level of understanding. Refusing to budge from the points of view we start with is anything but scientific. We stay, for the time being, with those axioms and principles that seem most consistent with observable reality, and we move beyond those that do not. Practicing science requires a willingness to give up on those outlooks that are consistently and convincingly disconfirmed by tests conducted under a range of circumstances in a variety of settings.

SOCIOLOGY AS SCIENCE

Theory *by definition* offers ways to explain variation in the things a discipline cares about. Sociologists care about the way people are interconnected with each other through direct attachments (face-to-face associations), shared beliefs (widely held concepts of what is appropriate and inappropriate, for example), and systemic interconnections, including regulatory constraint (as in the case of the subordination of citizens to laws). Readers should finish this book having a tool kit of axioms and principles that can be used to understand why direct attachments, shared beliefs, and systemic interconnections, including regulatory constraint (a) assume different shapes in different places, (b) produce ramifications people have to deal with, and (c) can, in some instances, be modified or reengineered to produce better outcomes.

Sometimes, people get the idea that "theory" really means "complexity" or "confusion." Believing this is equivalent to thinking that if a book is really obtuse, in other words, if you read it and reread it and reread it again and are still unable to figure out what the author means, it *must* be good theory. Well, wrong. Being obtuse does not make for good theory or good science. Good scientific theory is supposed to reveal things rather than obscure them. At its best, the elegance of theory is in its simplicity. Clarity of understanding is a science goal. Even though the world is a complex place, real theorists (in a science sense of the term) want to make things as clear as possible, not the opposite. It is, of course, true that we have to be prepared to suffer some confusion on our way to revelation. But revelation is nevertheless the goal. This book strives to identify and make clear (and ready for application) core insights for understanding interpersonal (micro), organizational (meso), and societal (macro) phenomena.

Good theorists are, almost by definition, out ahead of the crowd, so expect theory to be hard. But when this book reviews theorists who wrote long and, to the new sociology student, confusing works, the goal will be to decipher *core* insights and relay *core* contributions in a clear way. And when we are studying theorists who died a long time ago, people who at first glance may seem like relics of the past, our goal will be to appreciate the contemporary relevance of the ideas they advanced. When a dead person is discussed in this book, it is because he or she articulated ideals that have withstood the test of time.

A WORD OF WISDOM

In any science, theory has its greatest value when it offers insight that can help us better understand how the world around us operates. The ideas examined in this book meet that standard.

SOME VOCABULARY OF SCIENCE

This textbook considers theory within the context of science. Knowing the meanings of some key science terms will help keep the role theory plays in science fully in view. This is crucial. Theory has the importance it does because of its role within the framework of science.

SOME TERMS TO KNOW

Axiom. An axiom is the assumption that a given trait is common to all cases of a particular analytical type (e.g., all people, all organizations, or all societies). For example: All people try to maximize their own personal advantage. This axiom will be introduced more formally and more precisely in chapter 2 as the Rational Choice Axiom: *People tend to make benefit-maximizing decisions based on their priorities.* When some quality or characteristic is presumed to be present in all cases, and when we use that presumption to reason other things out, it is an axiomatic assumption. In good science, we try recognize and identify the assumptions we build into our conceptual frameworks. To say that a person uses an axiom when theorizing is simply to say that she assumes all units are alike in some particular way. It is very important to try to acknowledge the assumptions we make when theorizing so that we are conscious of them and can weed out those assumptions we are unable to justify. Acknowledging assumptions also helps us recognize when we are treating as given things we should be trying to explain.

Indicator. An indicator is a measurable piece of information used to gauge some more abstract concept. For example, income measured in dollars is often used to gauge differences of magnitude in economic class. Note that the validity of an indicator, in other words, the extent to which an indicator measures what it is purported to measure, is always open to question.

Principle. A principle is a hypothesis stated at the level of generic concepts. An example is a principle drawn from the work of Georg Simmel,[2] which will be discussed in more detail in chapter 3. The Conflict/Cohesion Principle is that: *Other things being equal, cohesion within groups increases as a function of the degree of conflict between groups.* This principle can be applied to very different units of analysis (college sports teams, nation–states, etc.) and is relevant in widely different time periods and circumstances. Yet, even when applied in dramatically different settings and under very different conditions, this principle has clear enough meaning to be useful for predictive purposes precisely because it is stated at the level of generic concepts (cohesion, conflict).

Independent Variable. A hypothesized cause.

Dependent Variable. A hypothesized consequence.

Research Hypothesis. A hypothesis stated at the level of measurable indicators, making an empirical test possible. For example: As hostilities between two countries intensify, the display of national flags and other patriotic emblems can be expected to increase within each country. In other words, if our principle is correct (if it is true that the greater the level of conflict between two groups, the more likely it is that the level of cohesion within each group will rise) then one should expect the display of flags to increase after international hostilities intensify. No single test of the research hypothesis would "prove" or "disprove" the principle, but a test of a research hypothesis can produce confirming or disconfirming evidence that strengthens or weakens our conviction that the principle is useful.

Micro-Level Phenomena. Those dealing with face-to-face interaction. Arguments between close friends are examples.

Meso-Level Phenomena. Those dealing with organizational phenomena. Trying to explain why decision-making authority is concentrated at the top of some organizations while discretionary authority is granted to lower-ranking operatives in other organizations is a matter of meso-level inquiry.

Macro-Level Phenomena. Those dealing with societal-level phenomena. Why divorce rates are higher in some countries than others is a macro-level question.

Science. Effort devoted to developing, testing, and refining explanations of variation in the real world, in search of a progressively better understanding of the way the world works.

> *Metatheory.* A conceptual framework consisting of orienting questions, sensitizing concepts, and the axiomatic assumptions that guide our thinking.
>
> *Theory.* Metatheory supplemented with predictive principles that enhance our ability to explain why cases differ and to consider ways of effectively implementing change.

These concepts are all necessary to encapsulate a standard science view. Research is used to test competing theoretical ideas that might explain how the world works. This means theoretical activity and research activity are parts of the same process, encapsulated by the scientific method. Neither theoretical activity nor research activity has its full value in isolation. Good research is grounded in theory and guided by theory, in the hope of ultimately improving upon and moving beyond the current state of theory.

THE CONNECTION BETWEEN THEORY AND RESEARCH IN SOCIOLOGY AS A MULTIPLE-PERSPECTIVE SOCIAL SCIENCE

When conducting research, it is important to be aware of the main bodies of earlier work and the central questions of a discipline, which attract the greatest amount of attention. Peter Blau and Otis Dudley Duncan's test of job success is a perfect illustration.[3] Before Blau and Duncan did their research, sociologists were divided in their understanding of inequality in the United States. Some sociologists firmly believed that America was a meritocracy, where the smartest and hardest-working individuals moved ahead occupationally, while lazy and dumb people slid behind. Other sociologists believed that the United States was a society based on ascription, with the outcomes of each person's life tightly constrained by the circumstances of his birth. The big question Blau and Duncan addressed was: *Is the United States actually a meritocracy, or is it a place where socioeconomic status is inherited rather than earned?* Their work had impact because they focused on an important question, and because they were very explicit in identifying this important question for their readers and conducting a reasonable test using data that was carefully gathered.

Blau and Duncan found that there is enough truth to both points of view (meritocracy and ascription) that both have to be taken seriously by people who are scientifically inclined, that is, people who raise questions about cause and effect and reach tentative conclusions only after careful consideration of available data. The research Blau and Duncan conducted convinced sociologists that our understanding of the real world should be informed by more than one theoretical point of view. Multiple perspectives (in this case ascription, drawn form conflict theory, and achievement, drawn from structural–functionalism) do not invalidate each other so much as they inform us about different dynamics at work. Blau and Duncan's research led them to draw from sociology's different theoretical perspectives rather than blindly privileging one perspective and ignoring the others. Indeed, years of research following Blau and Duncan have affirmed conflict theory by helping all sociologists better appreciate obstacles to mobility, at the same time that those years of research have affirmed structural–functionalism by identifying ways in which educational and other institutions have developed to promote the general betterment of society while providing structural avenues for individual advancement.

It is good to remember that the best scientific research often poses competing possible explanations. Considering more than one explanation in the same model helps us to refine and improve our understanding instead of merely validating our presuppositions. Improved understanding is more likely to emerge from an empirical test of a multiple perspectives model than from a single perspective approach.

RECAP

This chapter dispels a lot of myths about science. Science has less to do with memorizing inflexible formulas than it does with devising creative ways to test compelling ideas. And theory has less to do with philosophical complexity than with a culture of evidence that helps us reveal practical insights. In the process of working through this material, the reader has gained some exposure to four of the most influential sociologists who have ever lived: Robert K. Merton, Georg Simmel, Peter Blau, and Otis Dudley Duncan. Merton was a conceptualizer who brought the concepts of the self-fulfilling prophecy, role model, and the focus group into use. Simmel helped us recognize that solidarity among people often increases when they are faced with an outside adversary. And Blau and Duncan helped conduct research on status attainment that reminded sociologists that the best explanations are typically informed by insights drawn from more than one theoretical point of view.

NOTES

1. Robert K. Merton, *Social Theory and Social Structure* (Glencoe, Ill.: Free Press, 1968).
2. Georg Simmel, *Conflict and the Web of Group Affiliations* (1908; reprint, New York: Free Press, 1968).
3. Peter Blau and Otis Duncan, *The American Occupational Structure* (New York: Wiley, 1967).

CHAPTER REVIEW TEST

Test yourself with these questions and check your answers before moving on. The answer key is at the end of the book.

1. An academic field that is devoted to using observations of the real world in trying to develop explanatory frameworks that not only describe but actually explain variability is called a _____ .
     Science

2. What distinguishes sociology from natural and life sciences is its focus on:
    a. the way people are interconnected with one another in a face-to-face manner
    b. the nature of beliefs people share
    c. indirect systemic interconnections, including regulatory constraints
    d. all of the above
    e. none of the above

3. Ideally, scientists:
    a. try to prove the presuppositions they start their research with
    b. want to move beyond current understanding and improve our ability to explain variation between cases and/or change over time

c. reject the claim that anything about society can be better explained

4. What do macro, meso, and micro phenomena relate to? (Write "micro," "meso," and "macro" in the appropriate spaces below.)
   a. Having to do with interpersonal dynamics: _Micro_
   b. Having to do with organizational dynamics: _Meso_
   c. Having to do with society dynamics: _Macro_

5. Metatheory contains:
   (a) axioms but not principles
   b. principles but not axioms
   c. axioms and principles

6. Theory contains:
   a. axioms but not principles
   b. principles but not axioms
   (c.) axioms and principles

Check your answers in the answer key at the end of the book. If you get any wrong, reread chapter 1 and try to understand the reasoning behind each question and answer before continuing on to the next chapter. It is important to be clear about these questions before moving on, because they reflect the logical grounding that people need to have in order to understand sociology as a social science and begin to explore the predictive power of sociological theory.

APPLICATION EXERCISE

Each chapter of this book will conclude with an application exercise. These application exercises are only illustrations and should demonstrate that theory conveys insights that can be usefully applied. Always remember that science revolves around the *explanation of difference.*

An Empirical Question to Think About for a Moment: How do you think the majority of Iraqi people feel about the United States?

One Theoretical Question to Ponder: What explanations can we arrive at for explaining why Americans would have a range of sincere but different answers, rather than a single answer, when asked about Iraqi sentiment toward the United States?

Staying Focused on What You Are Being Asked to Explain: Sometimes it is hard to stay focused on what we are asked to explain. This is one such instance. We know that many people in the United States think most Iraqis love the Americans, and we also know that many people in the United States fear that most Iraqis despise Americans. It would be very easy (and very interesting, too) to fall into debate about who is right with regard to the empirical question of how most Iraqis really feel about the United States. But the theoretical question you are asked to focus on is: What explains the fact that Americans have reached a *variety of different conclusions* about what Iraqis feel?

Generating Explanations: Think of different ways this variation might be explained. One explanation might have to do with the relationships different Americans have with people who fought in the war in Iraq. One American might have a relative who fought in the war and returned home safe; another American might have a relative who died in the midst of the war; and yet another a relative who survived the war but was killed during the occupation. Still other Americans are of Iraqi ancestry. Some have relatives who died fighting to protect their own soil from people they regarded as foreign invaders, while other Americans of Iraqi ancestry have relatives who languished in jail as political prisoners before the arrival of the Americans. Differences in the experiences of those one knows personally might well have something to do with the fact that Americans do not all share the same perception of Iraqi sentiment toward the United States. Another possible avenue of explanation might have us consider sources of news. Over time, will the viewers of the Fox Network and the listeners of National Public Radio move closer to or farther from a common view regarding Iraqi sentiment toward the United States? Each of these news sources conveys news with a different emphasis and flavor. Does this difference in news coverage have consequences? And if so, what consequences? Yet another explanation might have to do with differences in the worldviews people are raised with. Some Americans grow up thinking that the United States has a completely altruistic foreign policy, and other people grow up thinking the U.S. government projects its power as a way of gaining access to raw materials and control over the flow of oil. If one is raised with a particular worldview, how does that shape the interpretation of subsequent events?

Ideally, offering testable hypotheses forces us to draw from, and encourages us to try to improve upon, our theories. Throughout the rest of this book we will learn about different bodies of sociological theory, always with an eye toward improving our ability to understand and predict events in the real world.

2

AXIOMS AND PRINCIPLES

Theory Is Not as Hard as It Sounds!

Sometimes, sociology students report being questioned about their choice of major by peers or parents. "Why are you studying sociology?" "What is sociology, anyway?" "What on earth are you going to do with a degree in sociology?"

Questions like these are easier to answer once you start using some axioms and principles. The terms "axiom" and "principle" seem awkward at first, but their meanings are fairly straightforward. More important, axioms and principles can convey a great deal of explanatory power. They show that sociologists really know some valuable things, and axioms and principles help distill sociological knowledge into a form that is easy to use. It is worth remembering that people as diverse as Ronald Reagan and Jessie Jackson were sociology majors as undergraduates in college. Each was very successful at what they did, in part because of their sociological skills and insight. That is what theory offers.

INTRODUCING AXIOMS

William I. Thomas, a sociologist writing almost a century ago from his base at the University of Chicago, where he conducted community studies in immigrant neighborhoods, pointed out that whatever people *believe* to be true tends to be real in its consequences. If a person fails to apply for a job because she is convinced there is no chance to get the job, then failure becomes a "self-fulfilling prophecy" (that very useful concept coined and popularized by sociologist Robert K. Merton).

W. I. Thomas's insight, which we can refer to as the Definition of Situation Axiom, is an axiom because it purports to identify a characteristic all people share. Thomas recognized that all people respond to situations on the basis of their perceptions about those situations. The "definitions of situation" an individual has can easily be wrong, but we still respond on the basis of what we think is happening.

Definition of situation was not something people thought about before the advent of sociology. Thomas came upon the insight while studying juvenile delinquents.[1] With the passage of time, sociologists have found again and again that Thomas was right. Among sociologists today, there is a lot of confidence in Thomas's Definition of Situation Axiom. Sociologists use this axiom all the time and it helps us understand the situations we encounter and observe.

Definition of Situation Axiom: *People respond to situations according to what they believe to be true about those situations, rather than what is actually true.*

Coming to a conclusion that all people are the *same* in responding to situations as they perceive them was extremely useful for Thomas as he tried to account for the fact that people react differently to what may appear to outsiders to be similar situations. Why does one person laugh when made the target of a joke, while another person lashes out in anger? We all know it depends, at least in part, on what the person thinks is going on. Is the joke *interpreted* as a sign of affection and inclusion, or is it *interpreted* as a sign of derision and disrespect? Definition of the situation matters very much.

It should be remembered that a person's interpretation is not always clearly expressed. It may even be subconscious. For example, the perception of threat elevates heartbeat (the "fight or flight" response) even before a person has time to consciously process what she thinks is happening. But whether conscious or subconscious, with full or only partial awareness, verbalized or not, it seems clear that the way people define things has a big impact on their reactions, and being alert to this offers social scientists a very powerful tool for understanding human affairs.

One should stop to consider this for a moment. People offer explanations for the behavior of others all the time. People offering explanations for the behavior of others often fail to take into account the situation as it is understood from the point of view of the person whose actions are being explained. When this happens, there is a high probability that the explanation is wrong, no matter how convincing it might seem. But it is almost never a sociologist making this mistake. The Definition of Situation Axiom is, in fact, part of sociology's stock knowledge. "Stock knowledge" is a useful term, referring to things people in a particular group take for granted that other people in the group know and appreciate. Sociologists can safely assume that other sociologists understand what "definition of situation" is and are aware of its importance.

Before moving on, try to think of a case in which someone (either yourself or someone else) reacted in a way that the person later regretted because he or she failed to consider the definitions of situation of other people. Most sociologists find it very easy to apply the Definition of Situation Axiom to real events. When we allow ourselves to be informed by the Definition of Situation Axiom, many things become clear that are otherwise hidden from view. Readers are urged to apply this axiom, and all the other axioms and principles in this book, to real cases and events. Sociological axioms and principles will then take on richer meaning.

Another important sociologist was George Homans, who built a series of explanatory principles based on an assumption that people make rational choices about how to maximize benefits in light of their priorities. We can call our presumption that all people seek to maximize their own interests the Rational Choice Axiom.

Rational Choice Axiom: *People tend to make benefit-maximizing decisions based on their priorities.*

People often calculate costs and benefits when deciding what to do. The Rational Choice Axiom simply introduces the premise that all people are benefit maximizers. When introduced as an assumption, benefit maximization can be used to deduce that people who make different choices must either face different circumstances or have different priorities. Then we can start asking interesting questions about, for example, why some college students work a lot of hours in paid employment while others do not. Perhaps this is because circumstances differ. Not all students are generously supported by parents, but some are. That is a matter of circumstances. But there are also questions of priorities. Learning is terribly important to some students, more important than almost anything else. But there are also students who deeply hunger for status-generating possessions (such as the "right" clothes) that cost money. Moving beyond axioms to account for variation between cases requires the development of explanatory principles.

Homans was a very smart person and realized that the Rational Choice Axiom was only a beginning. He recognized that sociologists would eventually have to answer the question: Why do people value what they value? For example, why are some people more altruistic than others? Homans was unable to answer this question, and he left the matter for a later generation of sociologists to address. But Homans was able to help codify our thinking about calculation, and in this respect his work provides sociologists with a useful principle introduced in the passages that follow.

INTRODUCING PRINCIPLES

Homans's work provides a particularly good illustration of sociological theory, because he was very conscious in his use of axioms and principles, and he was explicit in his desire to move beyond *axioms* identifying what cases have in common by stating *principles* that can be used to predict and explain differences developing between cases. This is clear in much of his work, but is best illustrated in his book *Social Behavior, Its Elementary Forms*. In that work, Homans makes a very clear leap to a principle when he recognizes that the more desirable a person judges something to be, the more the individual will sacrifice to achieve that object. This suggests a principle because it explains variability. Using an independent factor that varies from situation to situation (some ends are viewed as more desirable than others) allows us to predict variation (either case-to-case variation or variation over time in a single case) in a dependent variable (investment of time or money or effort in pursuit of an outcome).

Homans also codified a number of other principles, broadly drawn from the work of economists (especially economists who moved over to sociology, such as Vilfredo Pareto, who was the subject of Homans's first book) and of psychologists (especially his friend and colleague, the famous behavioral psychologist B. F. Skinner). The more confident someone is that a particular action will be rewarded, the more likely the person is to do those things that seem to be rewarded. People select among alternative lines of conduct by factoring in the probability of achieving desired outcomes, along with the value associated with those outcomes, and the projected costs of that course of action. These calculations are then compared with possible alternative courses of action by contrasting expected cost/benefit ratios. People weigh probabilities when they decide whether to be content with small gains that they consider to be almost certain or to try for bigger gains that seem less certain.[2]

It is legitimate to refer to Homans's work as true theory, because it represents an explicit attempt to explain variability in outcomes. The Rational Action Principle is at the center of his explanatory framework.

Rational Action Principle: *Other things being equal, the higher the value assigned to a goal, the lower the expected cost of a plan to achieve that goal, the greater the probability of success of the plan, and the less attractive are projected cost/benefit ratios of possible alternative courses of action in pursuit of this or other goals, then the more likely a person is to implement the plan under consideration.*

Homans and others have considered the implications of this elementary exchange principle and have arrived at a number of secondary principles that are quite revealing. For example, Homans notes that anger often results from a shortfall between expected an actual outcomes.[3] Where a student who expects a D actually gets a C, the person is rarely angry. But a student who expects a B and gets a C can be quite angry. Of course, whether the initial expectation is reasonable is a separate issue.

Anger Principle: *Other things being equal, anger increases in magnitude as a function of the degree to which actual outcomes fall short of expected outcomes.*

A great feature of abstractly stated principles is that they really are generic enough to apply to many different kinds of situations. We have already considered grades. Family income may offer another illustration. Some married couples draw apart because one person believes things are getting better over time (for example, feels accomplished because there is some growth in household income), while the other person judges the improvement to be a failure because it falls short of the rate of improvement that individual had projected. "Yes, you now make twice as much money as you did ten years ago when I married you, but if you weren't so incompetent you would be making four times as much money by now! How can you expect me to feel any passion for someone as incompetent as your meager income trajectory proves you to be?" Ouch!

Chapter 2

In real life, few things are so simple that they can be entirely reduced to the dynamic captured in a single principle like the Anger Principle. Nevertheless, the Anger Principle is one of the dynamics at work in many settings, and it goes a long way toward helping us understand what transpires in some of those settings.

WHAT PART OF DOING SOCIOLOGY IS DOING SOCIOLOGICAL THEORY?

In any science, people are doing theory when they are trying to better explain processes through which conditions change or different outcomes are generated. Theory is the attempt to identify dynamics producing variations in the world. If you cannot identify what you think might be the processes through which changes are generated and differences are produced, you have more theory work to do. Thoughtful effort to understand the dynamics producing change, and then to use observations of the real world to test and improve our understanding of those dynamics, is what defines any science. What makes sociology distinctive is its preoccupation with the social universe of interpersonal attachments, shared beliefs, and systemic interconnections, including regulatory constraints. In other respects, sociology is fundamentally like every other science. The difference is that it has the social world (the whole social world) as its subject matter. Good sociological theory will always offer some explanation of why social attachments, shared beliefs, and complex systemic patterns differ from place to place or change over time, and good sociological theory will provide us with insights about the consequences that might result from different kinds of attachments, different systems of belief, and different patterns of systemic interconnections and constraints.

In science, our goal is to move, at least in limited ways, beyond "common sense" viewpoints representing whatever has become the conventional wisdom of the times. And we ultimately want to improve on and move beyond whatever views we happen to have right now. There is nothing more antithetical to the idea of science than simply miring ourselves more deeply in the opinions we have always had.

RECAP

In this chapter, we have looked at ideas advanced by two of the most influential sociologists who ever lived: George Homans and W. I. Thomas. Both went on to be presidents of the American Sociological Association.

Each has been widely cited for more than a half century. Homans's work provides some of the pivotal foundation for exchange as a theoretical perspective in sociology (explored in chapter 14), and Thomas's work provides some of the pivotal foundation for symbolic interaction as an explanatory perspective (discussed in chapter 13). True to the promise of this book, important ideas having explanatory power are made clear, easily accessible, and available for readers to use. What we mean when we use the terms "axiom" and "principle" should now be clear. And the utility of being explicit about our theoretical axioms and principles should be more apparent with each passing chapter. Approached in this way, sociological theory is really not very difficult. But it *is* incredibly versatile and useful.

NOTES

1. William I. Thomas, *The Unadjusted Girl* (Boston: Little, Brown, 1923).
2. George Homans, *Social Behavior, Its Elementary Forms*, 2nd ed. (New York: Harcourt, Brace, Jovanovich, 1974), 43.
3. Homans, *Social Behavior*, 37.

REVIEW OF AXIOMS AND PRINCIPLES IN THIS CHAPTER

Definition of Situation Axiom: *People respond to situations according to what they believe to be true about the situation, rather than what is actually true.*

Rational Choice Axiom: *People tend to make benefit-maximizing decisions based on their priorities.*

Rational Action Principle: *Other things being equal, the higher the value assigned to a goal, the lower the expected cost of a plan to achieve that goal, the greater the probability of success of the plan, and the less attractive are projected cost/benefit ratios of possible alternative courses of action in pursuit of this or other goals, then the more likely a person is to implement the plan under consideration.*

Anger Principle: *Other things being equal, anger increases in magnitude as a function of the degree to which actual outcomes fall short of expected outcomes.*

CHAPTER REVIEW TEST

Check your answers in the back of the book. If you get any wrong, reread chapter 2 and try to get comfortable with the themes of the chapter before doing the workbook exercise.

1. A statement that asserts something is more or less true in all cases (e.g., people always want to elevate their status) is a/an:
   a. axiom
   b. principle
   c. research hypothesis

2. According to the Rational Action Principle, when people make rational choices about how to spend their time or money or reputation, they weigh:
   a. the benefit they expect to receive
   b. the costs they think will be involved
   c. neither of the above
   d. both a and b

3. All sciences involve a search for:
   a. more accurate description
   b. more convincing analysis of causes
   c. more accuracy in anticipation of consequences
   d. all of the above

4. Which of the following has a dependent variable and at least one independent variable stated at the level of concepts?
   a. an axiom
   b. a principle
   c. a research hypothesis
   d. a poem

5. The goal of science can be most accurately described as:
   a. seeking validation of theories we believe
   b. empirically testing predictions based on theory so that we can refine and improve theory over time

APPLICATION EXERCISE

Think about a situation in which someone (either you or someone else) got angry. Consider what happened. What events resulted in this anger, including the buildup of anger if that occurred? Try to be accurate and reflective. Where do you think this anger came from? Principles are written with the caveat "other things being equal." In other words, no single factor tells the whole story. If you were to try to improve upon the Anger Principle with a principle you were to write, what would that principle be?

3

SOCIOLOGICAL THEORY AND THE SCIENTIFIC METHOD

Science Is Supposed to Test and Ultimately Transform Theory

The *sciences* aim to increase our understanding of the world by improving theory. This scientific approach, based on *increasing* understanding by improving theory, is shared across all the sciences. All employ the same basic scientific method. This method can be described as having five steps. Followed in sequence, the steps in the scientific method provide a strategy for developing a better understanding of how differences are produced, which in turn makes it possible for us to develop more accurate predictions, and under the best of circumstances enables us to engineer better outcomes.

STEPS IN THE SCIENTIFIC METHOD

The first step in scientific method is to identify some difference between cases, or else some change over time within a single case, that seems worth trying to understand and explain. This step in the method is very important because it defines our focus. Remember that to be sociological, our attention needs to be riveted on some aspect of interpersonal attachments, shared beliefs, or systemic interconnections, including regulatory constraints.

The second step is to suggest one or more theoretical axioms or principles that might explain the kinds of outcomes we are trying to understand. So to use the scientific method effectively, one has to understand what axioms and principles are. And remember that the best research often weighs competing axioms and principles.

The third step in scientific method is to identify one or more research hypotheses that should be true if the stated theoretical axioms and principles are in fact accurate and do apply to the type of phenomena under study. A research hypothesis applies a highly generic theoretical principle stated at the level of general concepts to a specific set of cases and conditions. It does this by replacing generic variables with concrete measurement indicators suited to a specific setting, so that a prediction can be made and then tested by looking for confirming or disconfirming evidence.

The fourth step is to actually test empirical research hypotheses by judging whether observable outcomes match predictions. This is the methodologically driven stage of research. We test research hypotheses by collecting the information we need to confirm or disconfirm the accuracy of predictions we make following our axioms and principles.

The fifth and final step in scientific method is to use the results of empirical research in order to rethink, and try to improve upon, whatever theoretical ideas drove the initial design of the research process. Good empirical research often empowers further theory construction, and it is important to recognize that this is the ultimate goal of science. We want to "stand on the shoulders of giants" by trying to add to and also correct flaws in our existing base of insights.

PRINCIPLES: ANOTHER ILLUSTRATION

Remember that a principle is simply a hypothesis stated at the level of concepts. In other words, it is a cause-and-effect statement of relationship suggesting that changes in one abstractly worded variable or set of variables (which can be manifested in a variety of forms in different settings) tend to have a predictable impact on some other abstractly worded variable. A good illustration is found in the work of Georg Simmel, who was one of the founding figures in German sociology. Simmel advanced the theoretical principle that, other things being equal, the greater the level of conflict between groups, the greater the level of cohesion within each of those groups. We can call this the Conflict/Cohesion Principle. It is just one of many revealing insights that can be found in Simmel's work *Conflict and the Web of Group Affiliations*.[1] Change in one abstract variable (conflict) leads to a predictable pattern of change in another abstract variable (group cohesion). Conflict and group cohesion are abstract in the sense that they are relevant in many settings and express themselves in many different forms. Hence, Simmel could use his principle to explain differences in outcomes in many different types of cases in a wide variety of settings and circumstances.

This point about the generic character of truly powerful and abstractly worded theoretical insights can be illustrated with the principle of gravitational attraction. The principle of gravitation asserts that the level of attraction between two objects is directly proportional to their combined mass and inversely proportional to their distance. This principle helps us understand why apples falling from trees land on the ground (a big combined mass and a short distance translate into irresistible attraction) while the moon stays in orbit around the earth (about 20 percent more combined mass, but with gravitational attraction muted by an average distance of about 250,000 miles, so that gravitational force is insufficient to counteract the moon's inertial force). In fact, gravity is strong enough to drag the moon along in its orbit, thereby helping to maintain its velocity and, consequently, helping to keep it in orbit.

Principles derive their power, in part, from the fact that they are generic enough to apply to many different things. Simmel's Conflict/Cohesion Principle offers a good social science illustration of this point. It is abstract enough to allow for application to many different units of analyses, ranging all the way from team sports to nations at war.

Conflict/Cohesion Principle: *Other things being equal, cohesion within groups increases as a function of the degree of conflict between groups.*

Statement of abstract principles allows us some flexibility at testing ideas in different ways in order to improve our understanding about the realities of the empirical world. Working from his Conflict/Cohesion Principle, Simmel would have been comfortable predicting (in other words, making the research hypotheses) that there would be an increase in the number of national flags displayed on the streets during a period when foreign hostilities are increasing. But he would also have been comfortable making a prediction that University of California at Berkeley's college sweater sales would increase more before a Stanford–Berkeley game than before a Berkeley game with the University of Washington at Seattle. Why? Because Berkeley and Stanford have a long-standing cross-bay rivalry.

CAVEATS TO MAKE WHEN TESTING PRINCIPLES

There are four caveats to make when testing principles. The first is that principles can and should be tested in many different settings, to assess their versatility and power. This is part of the scientific process. A lot of research is conducted by a variety of people in the scientific community to see just how pervasive and consistent the dynamic being studied really is. Simmel would have been quite happy with empirical tests of both the research hypothesis about national flags during periods of international tension and the research hypothesis about college sweater sales before games with rival teams. The fact that we can see Simmel's principle at work in many different settings suggests that his insight is robust. We can therefore have some confidence that it can be applied in other cases as well.

A second thing to remember when testing principles is that other professionals reviewing our research have a right to expect that we have been careful in constructing measurement indicators that really are *valid* indicators of the more generic variables identified as important by our principles. Measurement validity is very important. Clear conceptual thinking helps inform choice of good measurement indicators. The simple questions that always have to be asked are: Are we trying to measure the most relevant factors? Are we actually measuring what we think we are measuring? The caveat is that the indicators we use when testing research hypotheses have to be valid measures in order for conclusions about our theoretical principles to be sound.

A third thing to remember about testing principles is that each principle comes with an "other things being equal" caveat, whether that caveat is explicitly stated or not. Let us say that Berkeley hat and sweater sales shot up right before games with Washington for three years in a row. It could be that for three years in a row the Washington game happened to fall in the middle of the worst cold snap of the season. Low temperature, rather than intercampus rivalry, could have been driving hat and sweater sales. One *always* has to consider the possibility that other dynamics can be at work (whether we are aware of them or not) and might overshadow what we are looking for. We cannot always anticipate or control for all other relevant factors, and "other things being equal" is our way of keeping this important caveat in mind. When we can anticipate and measure other factors that might influence the dependent variable, we try to include them as control variables in our models. Inclusion of control variables allows for a more reliable test of research hypotheses and allows us to speak with more confidence in reporting on evidence for the research hypothesis "after controlling for" the alternative explanations experts believe we should consider or reasonable people might advance as plausible.

A final caveat is that part of the scientific outlook is that our theories are imperfect. In fact, research is exciting for scientists specifically because it helps us improve our theories, often by helping us better recognize limitations on the accuracy of theory in its current state. The goal of science is always to search for *better* understanding, which means moving beyond theoretical errors and shortcomings of the past.

GETTING A THOUGHTFUL START

It is usually true that research that turns out to be significant begins with a good question. Coming up with a good question is a feat of intellect. It requires conceptual work to think out what the pivotally important issues really are. The pivotal issues in sociology generally revolve around the creation, the validation, the maintenance, the transformation, or the demise of interpersonal attachments, shared beliefs, or systemic interconnections of various kinds. Sociological concepts that command most interest are the ones that help us recognize differences among attachments, shared beliefs, and systemic interconnections. A partial list of such concepts might include status, role, identity, class, market, network, vested interest, reference group, role model, authority, norm, value, formal structure, informal structure, vertical integration, centralization of power, and institutionalization.

THE ETHICS OF THEORY-DRIVEN RESEARCH

The ethics of theory-driven research are grounded in a spirit of open inquiry and a culture of evidence. Good science thus requires open inquiry and a culture of evidence. Whatever the views of a social scientist may be, we always need to subject our own beliefs to serious test. We do this by seeing if we can articulate principles that allow us to make a variety of different predictions that can be assessed through honest examination of the world around us. This outlook is at the root of German sociologist Max Weber's call for "value-free sociology."[2] We will return to Weber repeatedly in this book, because he is one of the most important figures in the development of sociology.

Some people misunderstand what Weber meant by "value-free sociology." He did *not* mean we should ignore what we believe is important when studying society. He did mean, however, that even though it is appropriate to let our passions influence what we choose to study, we should never allow our passions to blind us to the point that they dictate what we find. A scientific orientation suggests that we should hope to conclude research by better understanding (which is to say, understanding differently) the things we are passionate about. *Wanting* to conclude our work by validating what we originally thought, and wanting that too strongly, can lead a person off the path of the culture of evidence science is based on, and onto a path of self-deception and propagandistic deception of others. Self-deception is not good science. Ideological tests of truth are not the hallmarks of good science.

There are also other very important provisions in sociological research ethics. We protect the privacy and anonymity of our information sources and research subjects. We keep confidential information private. And sociology's code of ethics prohibits research we can reasonably predict will hurt someone. This means we avoid intentionally placing people, including ourselves, in embarrassing or compromising situations. Over the years, there have been some ethical lapses by people conducting sociological research, but thankfully, these have been few in number.

BEING MINDFUL: THE POSTMODERNIST AND ETHNOMETHODOLOGICAL CHALLENGES

This text is consciously written as a social *science* treatise. It both advocates and reviews sociology's search for testable principles that can guide us in our efforts to make a better world. This approach is predicated on assumptions common to all sciences, including the social sciences: (a) there are understandable dynamics at work in this world, (b) we can improve our understanding of those dynamics over time by following the scientific method, and (c) following the scientific method means, among other things, putting some version of our best available understanding into words so that we can subject it to ongoing testing and improvement over time.

The basic premises of scientific sociology have been questioned by people who wonder whether it is possible for sociology to get progressively closer to the truth. People who express skepticism about social science do make good points, and it is wise to be mindful of them. The most common contemporary expression of skepticism about science claims is found in postmodernist thought captured in works such as Jean-François Lyotard's book *The Postmodern Condition*, which is deeply suspicious of science claims about "knowledge" and "progress."[3]

Postmodernists recognize that the stories people convey and the descriptions they offer are laden with meaning and tinged with often hidden bias. Such bias can divert people's attention from reality. For example, the way in which some people speak and write about poverty can deflect us from seeing structural sources of inequality and abuse. Many postmodernists see the common "knowledge" of the day as little more than a heavy veil of ideological beliefs reinforcing and even validating long-standing forms of oppression. To the extent that this happens, the fictional, fabricated "knowledge" of the day is actually harmful to the degree that it allows ideology to become so thickly interwoven with daily life and culture that it becomes difficult to detect or deflate. With this in mind, many postmodernists worry, with good reason, that today's "truths," including social science "truths," may in fact be fictions that serve to perpetuate inequality and legitimate exploitation.

Postmodernists combat this by trying to "deconstruct" texts for the purpose of discovering the subtle and not so subtle meanings that are reinforced by what people read and how people speak. "Knowledge," which is not knowledge at all, but really amounts to layers of unfounded presumptions serving special interests over the general interest, is often accepted uncritically and can survive a long time without being exposed. "Deconstruction," aimed at revealing meanings that are infused into the construction of text, performs a very important social service.

The notion that whatever people come to view as "truth" actually amounts to fiction created by our use of oral language and written text is central to postmodernist understanding, and it can sometimes be interpreted as casting a cloud of doubt over all "knowledge" claims, including those grounded in science. The postmodernist fear is that knowledge claims grounded in science are particularly hard to counteract, because science offers a special kind of legitimation in our society. But although this sounds like an outright rejection of any science approach, it actually suggests a point of convergence where social scientists can embrace postmodernist insights and incorporate them fully into a conventional social science worldview. This convergence is possible for two reasons. First, postmodernist deconstruction rests squarely on the premise that some things that are "known" (postdeconstruction awareness) are more accurate than other things that are "known" (predeconstruction ideological myopia). To the extent that postmodernists accept that it is possible for some knowledge to be more accurate than other knowledge, and believe more accurate knowledge is preferable to less-accurate knowledge, then postmodernists and scientists share the same objective. Second, the postmodernist recognition that social fictions can be created and propagated raises standard science-style research questions. How are social fictions fabricated and perpetuated? And when and how are such fictions, once established, overturned? These are, of course, social *science* questions, but they reflect postmodernist concerns.

Most social scientists appreciate and accept the validity of the postmodernist words of caution. Sociologists need to recognize socially constructed fiction and have to participate in debunking rather than perpetuating it. Indeed, we should actively work to debunk social fictions. But these are necessarily social science concerns and not merely postmodernist concerns. Real science abhors falsehood the way nature abhors a vacuum. The propagation of social fiction as truth is antithetical to the very idea of science, just as the use of social fiction to demean and exploit people or hold them back is antagonistic to the humanistic concerns at the base of most social science. Social science is driven by an interest in helping shape a better world, a world in which every person has opportunity for self-actualization and development. The postmodernist perspective is a healthy reminder that we need to take our call to science very seriously. The hallmark of science is progressive improvement in our understanding of the way the world really functions so that we can work effectively for a sustainable future offering opportunity for everyone.

A theoretical perspective in sociology that some view as a forerunner of postmodernism is ethnomethodology. Ethnomethodology was pioneered at the University of California at Los Angeles by Harold Garfinkel, who argued that people can function only by fooling themselves and others into believing that there is a commonly understood social reality.[4] People make it possible for social life to continue, in essence, by conspiring with each other to maintain a collective fiction of shared reality. Garfinkel maintained that we do this by using certain people ("ethno") techniques ("methods," hence the term "ethnomethodology"). This can be illustrated by use of the phrase "you know." In everyday interaction, people use this phrase to help move interaction along by mutually validating without stopping to confirm that everyone really does have the same meanings in mind. If we agree not to test our assumption that there is a shared body of meanings, we can proceed to do things as if we do share a common body of meanings, even if there is only an illusion of common meaning.

Garfinkel found that when people fail to engage in activity to sustain a presumption that a common understanding is shared, interaction grinds to a halt. If you don't believe this, you might consider a simple mental experiment. Imagine that the next time someone says "you know" to you, you respond by saying "I am not sure I do know what you mean, so can you please explain it to me?" In essence, your reaction would challenge the existence of shared meaning. Reactions like this are generally not regarded as friendly, helpful, or constructive. Garfinkel and the ethnomethodologists he inspired understand how fragile the illusion of shared reality is, and also how important it is for it to be maintained if social interaction is to continue as usual.

A very useful technique for determining how people affirm and sustain a sufficient sense of shared reality to allow interaction to continue is to perform a "breaching experiment." In this sort of experiment, one calls commonality of understanding into question and then carefully records what gets done to repair damage and shore up that sense of shared reality. At one point, some of Garfinkel's students went home for a holiday and treated their parents like strangers. Everyone but Garfinkel was surprised how sharp the parental reaction was. When breaching events first occur, the natural response is to provide the person who has challenged the assumption of shared meaning a second chance to reaffirm the assumption, as if they have just said something incredibly uncool and are being given one chance to retract what they have said. But if the person does not get in line with the shared meaning rapidly, normal interaction breaks down.

Ethnomethodological work has gradually come to emphasize "conversational analysis" as a strategy for discovering how people sustain the presumptions of shared meaning that are a precondition to stability in everyday social life.[5] In this respect, the research techniques used by ethnomethodologists are rather similar to techniques used by postmodernists, although postmodernists normally focus on global outlooks that are perpetuated within a whole society, while ethnomethodologists point their gaze at the strategies individual people use to create sufficient background sense of shared meaning to allow a given face-to-face interaction to continue.

RECAP

This chapter concludes part I of the book. At this point, readers should have a clear idea what science really means. For many readers, this will mean having debunked some old ideas. Science does not have any ultimate truth. If it did, science would be pretty boring. Science is the search for understandings that get closer to explaining observable reality than the understandings we had before. This makes every scientist an explorer. This is exciting. Social sciences deal with the most difficult subject matter to understand, because we can't touch what lies between people or put it under a microscope. What lies between people is real. It is important in its consequences. And it is challenging to try to understand it. That is why sociologists love what they do. Those sociologists who challenge our understandings about what we think we know, like postmodernists and ethnomethodologists are inclined to do, are important players in our social science quest to arrive at a deeper understanding of how the social world functions. The science question is fun, exciting, and important. Right now, the planet needs more, rather than fewer, people with good sociological training.

NOTES

1. Georg Simmel, *Conflict and the Web of Group Affiliations* (1908; reprint, New York: Free Press, 1955).

2. Max Weber, *The Methodology of the Social Sciences* (New York: Free Press, 1949).

3. Jean-François Lyotard, *The Postmodern Condition* (Minneapolis: University of Minnesota Press, 1984).

4. Harold Garfinkel, *Studies in Ethnomethodology* (Englewood Cliffs, N.J.: Prentice-Hall, 1967).

5. Jack Whalen and Geoff Raymond, "Conversational Analysis," in *The Encyclopedia of Sociology*, edited by Edgar Borgatta and Rhonda Montgomery, 431–41, 2nd ed. (New York: Macmillan, 2000).

SOME TERMS TO KNOW

Theoretical Power. The ability of a single principle to inform us about a variety of different events occurring under a range of different circumstances.

Measurement Validity. The extent to which an indicator actually measures what it is purported to measure.

Other Things Being Equal. The caveat that many dynamics are at work in the real world, some of which our models may not take into account. The operation of those dynamics can overshadow what we are looking at.

Deconstruction. Careful examination of material (often written text, but sometimes conversation) to *reveal points* that are subtly communicated, privileged, and affirmed.

Conversational Analysis. Careful examination of communication (usually oral, but often written) in order to discover how people use words in order to do the work of achieving certain outcomes.

PRINCIPLE REVIEW

Conflict/Cohesion Principle: *Other things being equal, cohesion within groups increases as a function of the degree of conflict between groups.*

CHAPTER REVIEW TEST

Check answers in the back of the book. If you get any wrong, reread chapter 3 and try to get comfortable with the themes of the chapter before continuing on.

1. List the steps in the scientific method as they are enumerated in this book.

2. Write out Simmel's Conflict/Cohesion Principle to see if you re-member it correctly. *As conflict between 2 groups increases the cohesiveness within each group increases.*

3. The "other things being equal" caveat suggests that:
   a. an indicator does a good job of representing what a researcher says it measures
   b. other factors, not indicated in our principle, might be having an impact on the outcome
   c. a particular theoretical axiom or principle helps us to explain variation in outcomes in many different kinds of situations

4. What does Weber's concept of value-free research caution against?
   a. doing research on things we have strong opinions about
   b. doing research on subjects that are in the political arena
   c. designing research in order to "find" what we want to find

5. It is most accurate to call an "if *x*, then *y*" statement of relation-ship written about abstract properties that can be taken to assume many different forms and can be found in many settings a/an:
   a. axiom
   b. principle
   c. research hypothesis

6. What group of theorists focuses their efforts on trying to "decon-struct" texts in order to uncover meanings that are subtly im-plied, privileged, and affirmed?
   a. all sociologists

b. postmodernists
c. ethnomethodologists

7. What group of theorists focuses their efforts on trying to understand how people maintain the sense of shared meaning necessary to sustain continued interaction?
   a. all sociologists
   b. postmodernists
   c. ethnomethodologists

APPLICATION EXERCISE

Find a newspaper or magazine article or editorial note or opinion piece that employs words in a way that seems to privilege certain viewpoints by encouraging people to accept, without evidence or discussion, some important points that may in fact be open to challenge. Begin to "deconstruct" this article by identifying the most questionable view that you feel is being propagated as "fact," to be accepted uncritically and without question.

Part II

Sociology's Most Prominent Founding Figures

Having completed part I of this book, readers should understand what axioms and principles are and how social scientists can use them. Part II examines what sociologists have come to appreciate as the intellectual foundations of the discipline. I draw from the works of Emile Durkheim, Karl Marx, Max Weber, and George Herbert Mead, as well as sociology's urban ethnographers and a collection of economists (in addition to Marx and Weber) who switched over to sociology or otherwise influenced the development of sociological thought. More than anyone else, these people are considered the authors of sociology's classic statements, and they produced the discipline's intellectual foundation. Their legacy is both powerful and enduring.

In part II, we will examine some of the great sociological ideas generated by the founders of our discipline at the end of the nineteenth century and the beginning of the twentieth century. But first, some historical background is in order. Chapter 4 sets the stage for our treatment of sociology's founders by introducing the historical context in which sociology emerged.

Among the people who dreamed of a great new era, one in particular began to envision a time when leaders could engineer a better society by using tested sociological principles to inform better policies and programs, and he gave sociology its name. He was Auguste Comte (1798–1857) of France. The tradition Comte started really took definitive form in the work of Emile Durkheim (1858–1917) of France, who was the first person anywhere in the world to hold the title of "professor of sociology" (actually, "professor of sociology and education"). Durkheim's work forms much of the heart of sociology's intellectual foundation.

A distinctive part of sociology's foundation was emerging at about the same time in Germany, evolving out of the German school of historical economics and providing a counterpoint to the work of Karl Marx (1818–1883), who is remembered for coauthoring *The Communist Manifesto* with Friedrich Engels in 1848). Marx drew attention to the importance of the economic system and the patterns of class interests that every economic system seems to create. Marx recognized that persistent strains of conflict could follow along the fault lines created by differences in the intrinsic interests of different economic classes. But Max Weber (1864–1920) viewed the social world quite differently. He was impressed by the degree to which shared values could unify a society even when class divisions were pronounced. And Weber rejected Marx's position that the nature of the economy ultimately determined everything else about a society. For example, Weber believed the impact of religious doctrine on the flow of historical events to be quite significant. Other prominent German intellectuals were also involved in this discussion. They generated a repertoire of penetrating insights about the way historical events unfolded over time. Marx was an economist and Weber was an economist before switching to sociology. In coming to sociology, they raised questions that were too big for economics to answer. Several economists of that era who were interested in the "big questions" (people like Vilfredo Pareto and Thorstein Veblen) also switched to sociology or intellectually engaged themselves in the sociological discourse. They helped shape sociology into a discipline concerned with all features of society (not just the economy, or government, or prisons, or houses of worship, or family units).

Meanwhile, in the United States sociology was emerging in close association with psychology. At the time, American sociologists and psychologists were all focusing on the "self." But the sets of questions sociologists and psychologists raised about the "self" tended to be different. Sociologists used "self" as a window on group phenomena. What goes on among people in group settings, American sociologists argued, produces individual differences in self-concept. And self-concept has the importance it does in substantial measure because of its impact on group dynamics. Sociologists were asking, How is a person's sense of identity merged with that of the groups to which the individual belongs? And what consequences do self and identity have for group process? Sociologists centered at the University of Chicago, around the unassuming person of George Herbert Mead (1863–1931), were laying the foundations for our understanding of individual adjustment to, and impact on, the wider social world. At the same time and place, sociology's urban ethnographers were adding to our understanding of processes of change within communities. All together, these works provided sociology with a powerful and enduring intellectual legacy.

In sociology, standing on the shoulders of giants is easy because several of sociology's founders were true intellectual giants. They left us a rich conceptual legacy to benefit from, appreciate, and add to. That legacy is the subject of this book. And the "legacy" theme is most dominant in part II.

4

THE HISTORICAL CONTEXT FOR A SCIENCE OF SOCIETY

A Healthy Regard for the High Cost of Chaos

Early sociology was a European creation more than an American creation. The historical context in which sociology emerged explains a great deal about what the discipline was to become.

SCIENCE AND REVOLUTION IN EUROPE AFTER 1700

The scientific method described in chapter 3 was considered a revolutionary way of thought a few hundred years ago. Galileo, remember, was persecuted by the Catholic Church for his use of telescope observations to test the conventional wisdom of that time, that the universe revolved around the earth. We remember names of people like Francis Bacon, Galileo, and Copernicus because they helped set in motion a revolutionary (that is, *world changing*) commitment to serious scientific investigation of the physical and biological worlds. Their purpose was to better understand how the world works, with the thought that more knowledge would ultimately help people make the world a better place. Early successes in fields such as astronomy and anatomy encouraged later scientific study in fields such as chemistry and geology. The scientific method is an important part of our common cultural heritage as human beings. It forever changed the lives of every single person living on this planet.

By the late eighteenth and early nineteenth centuries, the scientific approach had been so successful that some people began to call for a scientific study of the social universe analogous to the physical and biological sciences. People of scientific bent were no longer content to restrict themselves to the use of scientific method in studies of things they could easily point at and touch, such as rocks, trees, and kidneys. Some began calling for the creation of social science. They were optimistic that society (economy, religion, sports, politics, law, popular culture) could be better understood through careful social scientific theorizing and through data collection designed specifically for the purpose of helping us test, challenge, and reformulate our ideas in search of a better understanding of real-world phenomena.

In that general time frame, European society was in the midst of convulsive change. The French and American Revolutions were manifestations of that upheaval. Feudalism was coming to an end and people clamored for more economic freedom and opportunity. Aristocratic privilege based solely on family status was being questioned, and in many places a person's social standing was being influenced more by personal achievement and less by attributes of birth. There was even a revolutionary idea that community decisions should be arrived at through a system allowing for open discussion of issues and for public policy made by democratically elected representatives of the people. These ideas were revolutionary in the sense that they tended to encourage far-reaching change. And these are ideas that continue to excite fervor up to the present day.

The French Revolution of 1789 is a particularly important historical precursor to the development of sociology. It followed just a few years after the American Revolution, and it embodied similar ideals of *liberté, égalité,* and *fraternité.* But the French Revolution took place in an older society in which the rich enjoyed more lavish lifestyles. In France, members of a relatively large and decadent elite bled a vast and destitute peasantry living in squalor. Those peasants had no frontier to escape to and the society therefore lacked the kind of "safety valve" the sparsely settled American frontier offered.

The extremes of wealth in combination with an absence of a safety valve resulted in a combustible situation. With the benefit of hindsight we can understand why, after the onset of the French Revolution, the situation quickly turned into a "reign of terror." Thousands of nobles and their allies were marched off for public execution by guillotine. This brought a relatively quick, and it was thought even humane, end to life by cleanly chopping off the heads of the accused, but it also made for a bloody spectacle. Because the guillotine severs all the veins and arteries running to and from the brain, execution by this method results in a high volume of blood spurting out all over. Lining up several people at a time for execution, which was not uncommon at the height of the French Revolution, quite literally filled the gutters of some French streets with veritable rivers of blood. Because of its association with mob rule that can turn violent, democracy came to be feared by some of the same people who longed for it. Many British and French intellectuals of the time came to fear the thought of mob rule turning violent.

Meanwhile, the technical achievements and commercial fruits of the age of science were beginning to make themselves felt in very visible ways. The case of the steam engine is particularly instructive. Initially developed in the 1770s and enhanced in later decades by improvements in boiler technology, steam engines powered the industrial revolution in the early nineteenth century by freeing factories from reliance on waterwheels to drive equipment and by making long-distance bulk transport possible through railroads and steamships.

With the factory system beginning in earnest, manufacturing expanded rapidly and started a chain reaction many places, especially in Britain. Textile factories needed wool and cotton, as well as workers. Big landowners in England and Scotland pushed subsistence-oriented tenant farmers off the land, in what are sometimes referred to as "the clearances." Landowners, after all, needed to make room for more sheep to produce more wool to feed more looms to generate more profits that made mill owners wealthier. Meanwhile, displaced farmers streamed into cities and accepted low-paying jobs in the factories. Textile mills were extremely profitable and production expanded rapidly, reducing prices and fueling demand for even more textiles, which led landowners to push more peasants out of the countryside. Those were bleak times for working people. Karl Marx, writing in England, predicted bloody revolution all over Western Europe. Many members of the English middle class were afraid that England might replicate the French "reign of terror." And the French middle class, with fresh and painful memories of the reign of terror, feared that it might happen again in France.

At the same time, the age of science was also bringing dramatic improvements in public health. For example, the first successful vaccination (which was for smallpox) was tested in 1783. And the simple discovery, in 1813, that cholera was a waterborne disease made it possible for cities to dramatically reduce death rates by discharging sewage into rivers far downstream from intakes for drinking water. All these science-based improvements resulted in exponential population growth. Perhaps 300 million people lived on Earth at the time of Christ. Approximately 600 million were alive at the time of Columbus. This means it took a millennium and a half for the world's population to double. There may have been as many as 750 million people when the first vaccination was developed—a 25 percent population increase in a little under three hundred years. Then, steady improvements in public sanitation lowered the infant mortality rate, more babies survived to adulthood to have children themselves, and exponential growth began. One billion people were alive on the earth by 1830, two billion by 1930, three billion by 1960, four billion by 1976, five billion by 1988, and six billion by 1999. Cities grew more rapidly than the countryside, while railroads opened isolated rural areas to commercial development.

SOCIOLOGY AT ITS BEGINNING: A RESPONSE TO THE FIRE ALARM OF SOCIAL CHAOS

Locating the moment of conception of sociology at a particular date in European history clarifies an important point. The world was changing with unprecedented speed. That change was tumultuous, and even very frightening, for many people. Sociology was born in the struggle to understand the consequences of all this change, to anticipate an uncertain future, and to help engineer a better life for people. In social science, there was hope for a better future. This hope was starting to take hold by the 1830s, just as the world's population hit one billion people and just as Auguste Comte began to gain followers with his call for establishing a science of society to be called "sociology."

And what did people then hope for? Remember that this was only a generation after the French Revolution. Many French intellectuals dreamed of a society engineered for peace and prosperity and harmony through tested sociological principles. In other words, they wanted *progress marked by bloodless and relatively painless societal transformation*. They wanted progress hand in hand with social stability. They understood that the line between civility and chaos could grow thin. Having had a recent taste of chaos, most knew that they did not want the barrier between civility and chaos to be breached.

FOUNDER EFFECTS: AN IMPORTANT LESSON

As already noted, one of the people who dreamed of a great new era of social progress guided by scientifically tested sociological principles was the individual who conceived of sociology as a science and gave the discipline its name. He was Auguste Comte (1798–1857) of France. Comte started a tradition that really took shape in the work of Emile Durkheim (discussed in chapter 5) and largely defined what sociology was to become.

Comte died well over a century ago. And yet his vision continues to inform us. This is in part because of the power of his ideas. It also reflects the fact that people widely recognized him as the first real sociologist and accepted his definition of what the discipline should be. His science vision advocated empirical test of principles in hope of uncovering useful insights that would enable us to structure a better world. That vision took root and has had lasting impact on the discipline. This illustrates the importance of founder effects and suggests a revealing axiom.

Founder Effects Axiom: *Those interests and concerns of founding figures that become active parts of institutional memory tend to shape the activities of others for a long time to come.*

A founder's ideas tend to have lasting impact like a residue that lingers. That lingering residue does tend to fade somewhat over time, and the period immediately after control passes from a founder to the next leadership generation tends to be a particularly telling moment of transition. Nevertheless, the Founder Effects Axiom is useful for reminding us of an important regularity. The first voice tends to resonate into the future. Why are founder effects more pervasive and longer lasting in some organizations than in others? To answer that question, we would have to develop a principle to add to this axiom. For now, suffice it to say that sociologists assume founder effects are real, and we know they are important to consider.

RECAP

When commitment to scientific sociology began in France, historical experience had led most people to want progress without chaos. Chaos can ravage a society, often bringing often indiscriminant harm. Comte wanted nothing to do with that. In fact, he hoped sociologists would learn enough to help society avoid that fate. This inspired a commitment to applying sociology's theoretical insights to problems. That commitment continues to characterize the discipline.

A TERM TO KNOW

Founder Effects Axiom: Those interests and concerns of founding figures that become active parts of institutional memory tend to shape the activities of others for a long time to come.

CHAPTER REVIEW TEST

Check your answers in the back of the book. If you get any wrong, reread chapter 4, thinking about it as you go, before moving on to chapter 5.

1. When sociology started in France, what chaos was it intended to avert a repetition of?

2. At what point on the world's exponential population growth curve was sociology established?
   a. long before the beginning of exponential growth
   b. shortly after the beginning of exponential growth
   c. long after the beginning of exponential growth

3. Which began first?
   a. the scientific revolution
   b. the French Revolution
   c. the industrial revolution

APPLICATION EXERCISE

Read Charles Dickens's *A Tale of Two Cities* or watch one of the film or television versions of the novel. Consider the depth of feeling some people living through times of upheaval might have about the importance of social stability. Add to this a sense of marvel at the machines and vaccines made possible by science. Reflect on the enthusiasm for scientific sociology in France as Comte's life was drawing to a close and Emile Durkheim's life was beginning.

EMILE DURKHEIM AND THE BIRTH OF SCIENTIFIC SOCIOLOGY

Many people place Durkheim at the top of the pantheon of sociology's founders. He translated Comte's vision into a compelling theoretical perspective and followed a research methodology specifically designed with sociology's subject matter in mind.

REMEMBERING COMTE

August Comte was raised in France in the early aftermath of the "reign of terror," when many people feared revolutionary social disorder. Comte advocated the scientific study of society and coined the term "sociology" to represent this study. He explained that sociology would be the most challenging of sciences—the "queen science"—partly because the complexity of the social world exceeds the complexity of the physical and biological worlds, where things are more tangible, and partly because sociology concerns itself with the subject matter of all fields of social organization (business, criminal justice, civics, religious congregations, and so forth).

Comte feared the possibility of chaotic social disintegration, but he hoped that the discovery of social scientific principles would allow social planners to engineer a peaceful and prosperous society.[1] Although he failed to generate any predictive principles, we still remember him for recognizing that sociology could be a science.

Comte played a crucial role in placing the problem of order (social stability) on the center stage of sociological concerns. Comte believed that the kind of social order that bestows benefits of peace and prosperity could not and should not be taken for granted. He thought sociology would eventually make a vital contribution to humankind by arming leaders with well-tested sociological principles they could use to shape the more peaceful, more prosperous, and more civilized world he hoped for. This, of course, puts a burden on every sociology student. It is the burden of honing skills and becoming more constructively engaged as a citizen, applying sociological insights wisely to help make a better world.

HARRIET MARTINEAU HEARS COMTE'S CALL FOR A SCIENCE OF SOCIETY

Harriet Martineau (England, 1802–1876) was one of the people who accepted Comte's call to develop a science of society. She translated much of Comte's work into English and also conceived of a way sociologists might actually conduct a scientific study of society. Martineau did this by using government data to tabulate aggregate statistics on subjects such as suicide. Part of her genius was in recognizing that such statistics could serve as indicators of society's well-being and could therefore be used in empirical research about the society as a whole (not just the individual people in it). Martineau's dedication to statistical measurement is widely recognized as having helped make contemporary social science possible.

Martineau's focus on suicide was a particular stroke of genius. She recognized that suicide rate would be a telling indicator about the broad condition of a society undergoing rapid urbanization and industrialization, and an especially telling indicator on those matters pertaining to social order that were of such concern to Comte. Martineau conducted sociology's first important empirical research when she discovered that suicide was indeed becoming somewhat more common with industrialization. Her work placed scientific sociology squarely on an empirical rather than a more purely speculative or philosophical footing, and it set the stage for Emile Durkheim's pathbreaking contributions, which would ultimately define the future shape of the discipline.

A FOCUS ON SOCIAL FACTS

Following Comte and Martineau, Emile Durkheim (France, 1858–1917) looked at the world in terms of "social facts," or patterns of belief and behavior that can be said to be true of groups rather than individuals. Social facts are often deeply instilled in people through socialization and enforced by the coercive power of social pressure. If we look at classrooms, for example, we can see remarkable similarities in the way people behave. And why? Many of the patterns of behavior we emit are first programmed through socialization and then enforced by the groups to which we belong.

The concept of social facts and the coercive force of groups is central to understanding Durkheim. Consider your choice of clothing today: your "choice" of what to wear and even your "choice" of whether to wear anything at all. Durkheim recognized that the social groupings we are part of impose certain decisions with the coercive force of social pressure. We must do certain things and we must avoid doing others because the consequences of disregarding group norms are more than most people can bear. Regarding most matters, the negative reactions of other people are simply much more than the average person wants to withstand.[2]

Keep definitions of situation in mind. If an American college student who uses ordinary language and travels in social circles where ordinary language is typically used suddenly starts using a lot of coarse "gutter talk" everywhere, that person's life is likely to start to change. Durkheim's point, which is certainly true and easy to appreciate, is that if a norm is deeply held and imbued with a lot of importance by the group, the group is quite capable of making defiance of the norm *very* uncomfortable and *very* costly. Groups are capable of asserting themselves with considerable coercive force about things that matter to the group. Group reactions of this kind are thoroughly stigmatizing. That is, as Erving Goffman emphasized in his 1961 book, *Asylums,* the reputation of a person can be thoroughly tainted in ways that are hard to overcome.[3]

Often, we don't recognize the coercive force the wider society exerts on us. This is because people so fully internalize norms that the average person automatically complies with them without stopping to think about them. But should we deviate, the weight of social compulsion can be burdensome indeed.

DURKHEIM ON SYSTEMIC INTERCONNECTIONS AND REGULATORY CONSTRAINT

Being intrigued by social facts, Durkheim began his career as a sociologist by trying to describe and explain variations among different kinds of soci-

eties. And as a sociologist he was particularly interested in variations relating to social attachments and shared beliefs. This is plainly evident in
Durkheim's first great book, *The Division of Labor in Society* (1893).[4] In it,
he noted that the urbanizing societies of Western Europe were structur-
ally changing in ways that had far-reaching consequences.

Durkheim's analysis in *The Division of Labor in Society* treats the law as
a body of social facts, or patterns of belief and behavior that are true of
groups rather than individuals. He noted, for example, that the relationship between victims of crimes and perpetrators of those crimes tends to
change when societies industrialize. Prior to industrialization, legal codes
seem to be dominated by a tone of moral outrage about transgression.
Societies tend to define justice as a mechanism for expressing moral outrage and extracting revenge for victims. But as industrialization proceeds,
Durkheim noted, law changes in a predictable way. The tone of moral
outrage subsides and is supplanted by a sense of mutual tragedy when
unfortunate things happen in a complex world. Emphasis is placed on
seeking justice through restitution to at least partially compensate a person for a loss. In every society, law extracts a blend of revenge and restitution. But Durkheim recognized the proportional mix in each society as a
social fact. As societies industrialize, the thirst for revenge to assuage
moral outrage subsides and gives way to the wish to move on after receiving partial compensation for loss, which normally results from events occurring under morally ambiguous circumstances. Thus, regulatory constraints are altered in predictable ways when the nature of the systemic
interconnections weaving their way through the fabric of society are
transformed. As specialized division of labor spreads, the body of civil
law grows in proportion to the body of criminal law.

The researcher in Durkheim worked to describe social facts in industrializing countries in contrast with preindustrial ones, and he did this by
identifying characteristics of legal codes. The theorist in Durkheim
wanted to explain variation between cases and change over time. Those
are two different activities. What excited sociologists most about *The Division of Labor in Society* was the structural–functionalist mode of theoretical
analysis Durkheim began to advance as an explanation for what he
found. Put simply, in society as in physiology, *form follows function*.

FORM FOLLOWS FUNCTION: EARLY
STRUCTURAL–FUNCTIONALISM

Why would a legal system change during industrialization? Durkheim's
answer to this question includes all the major ingredients of his sociology.

For societies to continue to cohere, they must be integrated in some way. Most people in preindustrial societies are semisubsistence agriculturalists. In terms of economic interdependence, there is little by way of systemic interconnections that integrates the whole society. So, Durkheim noted, where preindustrial societies are well integrated it tends to be through a system of shared beliefs, or "collective conscience" fostered by similarity of lifestyle and myths of common origin. Strong collective conscience involves uniformity of beliefs about good and bad and right and wrong, discourages questioning, and fosters a sense of moral outrage when people violate the rules everyone takes for granted. Vengeance as a form of justice mirrors a level of integration rooted in collective conscience, and it also sustains it by reaffirming common definitions of right and wrong. Punishment as a moral statement invigorates agreement about right and wrong if such agreement exists. It does so by reminding people that we have collectively defined some acts as "really bad," so bad that they need to be severely punished. So where economic self-sufficiency prevails, enlivening the collective conscience through occasional expression of moral outrage helps hold society together.

The use of symbols of affinity is something else that Durkheim recognized enlivens collective conscience. It does so by affirming group memberships and by reminding people what membership means. That was the subject of Durkheim's 1912 book, *The Elementary Forms of Religious Life*.[5] Sociologists like William Goode maintained this interest, stressing the importance of hero stories that celebrate not only group membership, but also special qualities the group values.[6]

With industrialization comes heterogeneity of lifestyles and what Durkheim termed as the *enfeeblement of collective conscience*. That is, lose some sense of common origin and a society tends to drift away from singular definitions of what's appropriate and what's inappropriate. What, then, integrates the society? Integration comes to be based on mutual interdependence. The division of labor, in Durkheim's view, is a structural form that satisfies the functional need for system integration in industrializing societies. But increased division of labor requires legal forms based on restitution rather than retribution, because complex relations grind to a halt at moments when large numbers of people are gripped with a sense of moral outrage. It is functional, therefore, for legal codes to change, putting legal emphasis on restitution rather than revenge. This led Durkheim to conclude that *form does follow function*. Things are done a certain way (form, structure) because it helps society work better (operational success, functional performance, integration, for example). Indeed, trying to extract vengeance where the collective conscience is enfeebled tends to turn people off. In the absence of a strong collective conscience, vengeance simply looks like cruelty.

DURKHEIM ON SUICIDE AND ON INTEGRATION AS A SOCIETAL FUNCTION

Emile Durkheim viewed himself as a social scientist. He wanted to develop explanations (theory) that he could empirically test (research). His most famous effort to do so was his 1897 book, *Suicide*.[7] Durkheim saw this subject as an opportunity to develop a strong research tradition in sociology building on Martineau's work in an effort to bring Comte's vision of scientific sociology to life.

Durkheim published *Suicide* utilizing government statistics to test a variety of hypotheses about suicide as a social fact, that is, about changes in and differences between suicide rates. Durkheim found that measures of social bonding or integration (for example, the number of people being uprooted in the urbanization process and the number of people practicing different kinds of religions) were highly correlated with suicide rates. But what is much more important from the vantage point of theory is that Durkheim gave us a series of powerful insights that amount to a very versatile explanatory principle that we can term Durkheim's Principle of Social Control.

Principle of Social Control: *Other things being equal, the more integrated the members of a group or community are (the more interconnected they are and the more bound they are to a common set of beliefs) and the fewer offsetting ties people have to other groups or communities, then the greater the level of social control the group or community will exert over its members.*

In part, Durkheim's insights derive from a typology he developed to distinguish among different sorts of suicide. This typology has had a lasting impact on sociology because it clearly embodies our commitment to the study of both (a) attachments (such as role relationships, network ties, and institutional connections) and (b) shared beliefs. Durkheim noted that too little of either kind of integrative connection within a group (either too little attachment or lack of clarity in shared beliefs) can lead to high suicide rates. Interestingly, these two types of suicide are recognizably different. "Nobody cares about me," which suggests lack of attachment, is different from "I don't know what a person like me is expected to do," which suggests a lack of clarity about shared beliefs. This discovery by Durkheim bore little resemblance to the commonsense ideas of his time. It was a new sociological discovery. The French book-reading public immediately recognized that sociology was able to offer rare insight, and sociology has remained a popular and respected field of study in France ever since.

Durkheim went further. He realized that just as too little group integration is associated with high suicide rates, a group that is very tightly integrated can also push members toward suicide to avoid serious embarrassment within the group or in a sacrificial act trying to defend the group against hostile outsiders. After the publication of *Suicide* in 1897, Durkheim turned his attention to guiding young researchers inspired by his sociological approach to understanding the world. In the years leading up to World War I, Durkheim's young research colleagues put out a steady stream of good work, much of it published in Durkheim's journal *Année sociologique*.

THE BEGINNING OF SOCIOLOGY'S SPECIAL RELATIONSHIP WITH ANTHROPOLOGY

Durkheim always kept integration in the center of his sociological analyses. His last great work, *Elementary Forms of Religious Life* (1912), explores the use of rituals and symbols of communion (often involving totems) in cementing groups together. Celebrating heroes, participating in rituals, and engaging in communion activities all help to solidify feelings of group membership and remind members what they stand for.

In a quirk of intellectual history, *Elementary Forms of Religious Life* was to mark a milestone in anthropological thinking. The most influential British social anthropologists of the day, Bronislaw Malinowski and A. R. Radcliffe-Brown, read Durkheim's structural–functionalist theory emphasizing that form follows function. They began applying Durkheim's structural–functional mode of analysis to what seemed to be exotic social patterns found in different cultures. And they arrived at new insight by asking what special function those patterns might have developed in order to perform for society. Following the lead of Malinowski in his 1922 book, *Argonauts of the Western Pacific,* anthropologists spent decades employing the structural–functionalist approach developed by Durkheim.[8]

THE BASIC STRUCTURAL–FUNCTIONALIST MODEL

To say that form follows function means that social patterns and structural forms develop to meet needs. This dynamic can be easily illustrated. After 1980, a lot of schools began to provide, or dramatically expanded, before- and after-school care for children. Structural–functionalists would have an easy time offering an explanation. As the number of single-parent households increased, and as the number of dual profession households continues to increase, unmet need for before- and after-school care began to mount. School systems offered a practical way of meeting at least part of that unmet need. At the time, had the United States had larger families, stronger extended family ties, less geographic mobility, a lower divorce rate, and fewer two-income families, most people would have had family alternatives to after-school care. Schools would have been under far less pressure to take on that task. But circumstances were otherwise. There was a need, and schools were in a position to do something about it. Thus the idea that form follows function offers a way of looking at the world that can be quite thought provoking.

Durkheim did not have a chance to develop his embryonic structural–functionalist analysis. Shortly after the publication of *Elementary Forms of Religious Life,* World War I broke out. Almost all of Durkheim's young protégés (including his only child) died in World War I, starting at the First Battle of the Marne in September 1914. In that battle, pitched resistance that halted the German advance on Paris helped save France from defeat and plunged Germany's western front into trench warfare. But the death toll among the small cadre of French sociologists was astronomically high. Durkheim, still a comparatively young man at fifty-nine, died brokenhearted in 1917. His work was known primarily in France, and it might have been lost to American sociology. But after World War I a number of American sociologists were reading British social anthropology, where they encountered Durkheim's framework and were impressed by its promise. Robert K. Merton was a particularly important conduit, exposing a group of Harvard sociologists who were to become central players in sociology from the mid-1930s through the 1960s (discussed in chapter 11).

EMILE DURKHEIM AND THE SCIENTIFIC METHOD
IN SOCIOLOGY

Emile Durkheim was an early and influential advocate of the use of scientific method in sociology. His study of suicide, first published in France in 1897, is a textbook illustration of scientific method in action. Reviewing Durkheim's examination of suicide helps clarify how scientific method came to be employed in sociology.

The first step in scientific method is to identify some difference among cases, or change over time within a single case, that seems worth trying to understand and explain. Durkheim, along with many other people in his era, identified suicide rate (not suicide as a singular event, but suicide *rate* as an aggregate societal indicator) as a variable worth studying. The focus on rate is critically important. Of course, sociologists were interested in what would drive an individual person to commit suicide. But their curiosity centered on why rates would be higher in some communities than others.

The second step is to advance a theoretical principle or set of principles that might explain the kinds of outcomes we are trying to understand. Durkheim began by considering the conventional wisdom of his time. In the late nineteenth century, psychological distress was generally advanced as the explanation of individual suicide, but many people applied this idea to the suicide rate of whole communities. The prevailing view seemed reasonable enough. Suicide rate was probably going to be highest in places and at times of mass distress, such as during an economic depression or after defeat in a war. Part of Durkheim's argument rests on an appreciation for the fact that certain things should be true if psychological distress really does offer a good explanation for variation in suicide rates. This brings us to some research hypotheses.

The third step in scientific method is to move beyond general discussion of what different people theorize to be true, by identifying (either quantitative or qualitative) empirically testable hypotheses that should be true if the theoretical analysis is accurate. Durkheim chose to look at quantitative statistical data for his analysis. One of the themes in Durkheim's book is that all nations go through periods of greater or lesser distress, and that suicide rates should therefore vary considerably over time within each country, assuming psychological distress is, more than anything else, responsible for variation in suicide rates. Of course, the times of greatest stress would occur in different years in different countries. The defeat of France in the Franco–Prussian war, for example, marked a much lower point for people in France than in the newly united Germany, which coalesced into one victorious nation–state after that war. Nevertheless, all countries and all regions within countries might be expected to have a similar range of high to low suicide rates across time, corresponding with good and bad times enjoyed by those countries. Hence, Durkheim had a set of easily testable hypotheses based on psychological disruption as an explanation of suicide rate. If distress offered a good explanation, the yearly suicide rate in any one country should go up and down rather dramatically over a period of years: down with good times and up with bad times. Reasoning this way, one might also expect that high and low suicide rates for different countries and regions would be roughly comparable in magnitude (at least for countries at somewhat similar levels of economic development), even though highs and lows would probably occur in different years for different countries.

The fourth step is to test empirical hypotheses thought to be consistent with the explanatory framework being tested. Durkheim tested his hypotheses in order to evaluate the utility of an explanatory framework based on psychological distress. The hypotheses were *not* confirmed. Most countries have suicide rates that are remarkably stable over time. Good times? Bad times? It doesn't seem to matter much at all. Rates in most countries do not go up or down very much from year to year, or even from decade to decade. Moreover, some countries (e.g., Denmark) consistently have high suicide rates, while others (e.g., Ireland) consistently have low suicide rates.

The fifth and final step in scientific method is to use the results of hypothesis testing in order to fuel theoretical reformulation. Durkheim did exactly that. After looking at patterns in his data, including higher suicide rates in cities than in the countryside and higher suicide rates in Protestant areas than in Catholic ones, Durkheim concluded that well-integrated communities tend to have lower suicide rates, as well as other forms of aberrant social behavior. Places where webs of social interconnections are less dense or where collective understandings are weaker will tend to have higher suicide rates. Integration matters. Durkheim formulated his insights about integration, summarized earlier as Durkheim's Principle of Social Control, which is a principle well worth learning. The power of Durkheim's analysis was instantly recognized by his readers at the time.

RECAP

Durkheim was a monumental figure who left a lasting legacy. That legacy stresses several points. First, sociology should be a science, using data to test and improve upon our understanding of the social universe. Second, groups, organizations, communities, and societies are more than collections of individuals. Communities, organizations, groups, and societies have characteristics that are not reducible to an aggregation of traits of individuals. Third, if we want to describe social structure, we have to do it in terms of both attachments (direct interpersonal attachments and systemic connections including regulatory constraints) and shared beliefs. Fourth, in groups, organizations, communities, and societies, form follows function. There is a connection between the social structure that develops and the systemic needs of the wider community. And fifth, social control increases with degree of social integration. To understand Durkheim's legacy is to really begin to understand sociology.

A concluding remark on the cumulative nature of science is in order. Keeping all our theoretical axioms and principles in mind can help us discover things. To use one example showing that theoretical axioms and principles can be applied to many different kinds of cases, and when applied can lend a lot of explanatory insight, consider the fact that some teenagers get in very serious trouble and others manage to avoid serious trouble. But all teens have to contend with roughly the same hormones. An explanation of differences in risk for delinquency has to consider the realities of peer pressure. But teens in different groups feel pressured to do different things. Teens whose peers get into trouble are themselves more likely to get into trouble. This is especially true if the teen has few countervailing influences because, as Durkheim's Principle of Social Control alerts us, the sway of a group will be greatest when the individual's countervailing ties to other groups are most tenuous.

Thomas's axiom about Definition of Situation and Homans's Rational Choice Axiom and Rational Action Principle can help us appreciate some of the behavior of "juvenile delinquents." If a person's definition of situation is that he is rejected outside of the peer group, then the individual will have very little "stake in conformity," or in other words there is little reason for following mainstream rules once it is presumed that acceptance into the mainstream is never going to happen. Under those conditions, conformity is viewed by many people in the youth culture, especially those from a low socioeconomic status background, as a goal only for "chumps." Keeping in mind all our axioms and principles and applying them thoughtfully yields real explanatory power.

Of course, perceptions that one has little stake in conformity are frequently wrong. It is very common for people to have more to lose than they think. But if one's definition of situation is that she has nothing to lose (by ditching school, for example), then that person's cost/benefit calculations will certainly be affected. The crisp insight we get by applying sociology's theoretical axioms and principles can be used to make sense of much of what happens in this world.

NOTES

1. Auguste Comte, *The Positive Philosophy of Auguste Comte* (1854; reprint, London: Bell and Sons, 1896).

2. Emile Durkheim, *Rules of Sociological Method* (1895; reprint, New York: Free Press, 1982), chapter 1.

3. Erving Goffman, *Asylums* (New York: Doubleday, 1961).

4. Emile Durkheim, *Division of Labor in Society* (1893; reprint, New York: Free Press, 1964).

5. Emile Durkheim, *Elementary Forms of Religious Life* (1957; reprint, New York: Free Press, 1951).

6. William Goode, *The Celebration of Heroes: Prestige and Social Control* (Berkeley: University of California Press, 1978).

7. Emile Durkheim, *Suicide* (1897; reprint, New York: Free Press, 1951).

8. Bronislaw Malinowski, *Argonauts of the Western Pacific* (New York: Dutton, 1922).

SOME TERMS TO KNOW

Social Fact. An attribute or pattern of belief and behavior that is true of a group or collective social unit.

Stigma. A belief about an individual that harms that person's reputation in a way that is hard to overcome and tends to limit the scope of interaction others are willing to have with the stigmatized individual.

Collective Conscience. A strong sense of membership and uniformity of deeply held agreement about what is considered good and bad and right and wrong.

Enfeeblement of Collective Conscience. A weakening in the sense of a common belonging group members have and an evaporation of any deeply held agreement about what is considered good and bad and right and wrong.

REVIEW OF PRINCIPLE

Principle of Social Control: *Other things being equal, the more integrated the members of a group or community are (the more interconnected they are and the more bound they are to a common set of beliefs) and the fewer offsetting ties people have to other groups or communities, then the greater the level of social control the group or community will exert over its members.*

CHAPTER REVIEW TEST

Check your answers in the back of the book. If you get any wrong, reread chapter 5, thinking about it as you go, before moving on to chapter 6.

1. What man is credited with conceiving the possibility of a science of society and terming it "sociology"?

2. What woman is credited with pioneering our study of suicide rates and treating them as social facts and as key indicators of the condition of a society?

3. Who is credited with initial development of structural–functionalist analysis, explaining the way in which legal systems changed with increased division of labor and then spending the balance of his career examining societal integration from a number of other vantage points?

4. What role do symbols play in organized social life?

5. Write out Durkheim's Principle of Social Control and an application of it.

APPLICATION EXERCISE

Think of Durkheim's Principle of Social Control with reference to groups pressuring people to conform. Consider an example you are familiar with. What does that example reveal about the power social groups exert over their members? Durkheim recognized that some groups exert more power over members than do other groups. The typical army platoon exerts more power over the thoughts and actions of platoon members than does the typical sociology class over class members. The Social Control Principle offers some explanations why. What are those explanations? Do you find them convincing? Then think of a social group you belong to. What kinds of behaviors and attitudes does that group encourage in its members? What kinds of social pressure are used to gain conformity to the forms of behavior and belief the group encourages?

6

MARKETS VERSUS OTHER FORMS OF ORGANIZATION

The Intellectual Backdrop of Early Sociology

Sociology is a comparatively young discipline. There was not a sociology class taught in the United States until 1875. That was taught at Yale University by William Graham Sumner. There was not a university teacher with the title of professor of sociology anywhere in the world before 1891, when Emile Durkheim, in France, was appointed a professor of sociology and education. There was not a free-standing department of sociology anywhere in the world until 1892, when one was established at the University of Chicago. But sociology did not just spring forth out of nothing. It was forged by an amalgamation of people who were working on the margins of several disciplines and united by their interest in a common set of issues. The intellectual parentage of sociology is to be found in economics more than in any other single discipline. Sociology has borrowed substantially from economics. In particular, exchange theory (to be examined in more detail in chapter 14) emerged out of and has moved forward from mainstream economics. Sociology has also bequeathed a great deal back to economics, although sometimes without receiving much credit. Much of what sociologists have learned about meso-(organizational-)level phenomena and macro-(societal-)level phenomena has been in response to inadequacies of conventional economics. Conventional economics is tremendously important. Where it works, sociologists use it. And when it does not tell us enough, sociological axioms and principles make up some of the shortfall.

MARKETS ARE PART OF SOCIOLOGY'S SUBJECT MATTER

There is nothing quite so central to sociology's intellectual history, and yet so frequently overlooked in treatments of sociology's intellectual history, as economic markets. First, markets are one of the main ways human interaction is organized. That makes them central to sociology. If sociologists were to ignore markets, we would be denying our own reason for existence as a discipline, which is to better understand how patterns of social organization and shared meaning are shaped and have consequence. Second, while economics primarily concerns itself with market operations, sociology is more encompassing and deals in equal measure with (a) markets, (b) hierarchies, such as government, and (c) networks, such as friendship cliques, information chains, and strategic alliances. Markets, hierarchies, and networks are fundamentally different structural forms. Third, sociology has the tremendously important task of helping us understand which form of organization will predominate over which geographic areas and spheres of activity. Fourth, while economics has a lot to say about the structure and operation of markets, and political science has a lot to say about the structure and operation of hierarchies, sociology is important in understanding all three (markets, hierarchies, and networks).

For sociologists, one pivotal question is: When will market organization prevail over hierarchy and networks, when will hierarchical organization supplant market and network organization, and when will network organization hold sway in the face of market and hierarchical forms of organization? But that is only part of sociology's special charge. Sociology takes account of ways that information can be distorted and choice can be limited, invalidating assumptions on which conventional economic thinking is based. The point is that conventional economic theory developed out of models about perfect markets. But it is the all-too-real market imperfections that sociology helps us to understand.

WHAT ARE MARKETS AS A FORM OF ORGANIZATION?

Economics is itself a comparatively new discipline. By far the most important figure in the history of economics as an academic discipline is Adam Smith, whose most famous work, *The Wealth of Nations*, was first published in 1776. Smith described markets and advocated the expansion of markets as a form of organization. In this respect, he advocated a kind of social revolution, for free markets would allow people to escape the constraints of tradition and habit.

People are now so familiar with the word "markets" that we sometimes fail to think about the fact that markets are a distinct form of social organization that was much less widespread two hundred years ago, when most human beings were subsistence agriculturalists who never strayed far from the place they were born, deviated much from the traditions they inherited from their parents, or broke from the constraining commitments of the neighborhoods where they led their lives. It is absolutely critical in the conceptual maturation of a sociologist to appreciate the fact that *a market is a form of social organization* and therefore is squarely in the central domain of sociological inquiry. Markets are not alien territory. A sociologist has to know what a market is and how it differs from other forms of organization, because markets are one of the most prevalent forms of social organization. Part of being a good sociologist is recognizing why markets actually perform better than other forms of organization under certain sets of circumstances and less well under other sets of circumstances.

What is a market? What distinguishes markets as a form of social organization? To satisfy Smith's conceptualization, a perfect market has to have four characteristics: (1) people must be engaged in exchange that can be at least loosely conceptualized as having "buyers" and "sellers" or "traders"; (2) there must be freedom of choice so that each buyer/seller/trader can decide who, if anyone, he wishes to trade with; (3) there should be "transparency," or ready availability of complete and accurate information, so that potential exchange partners can make informed decisions; and (4) "barriers" to entry into business need to be minimal so that a steady stream of new producers/traders can enter into competition. Many of Smith's views are captured in the Rational Action Principle, expressed earlier in this book.

Most people are familiar with the process as Smith described it. The "invisible hand of the market" following "laws of supply and demand" allows people to select among the best available options. Smith thought this would produce good results for almost everyone over the long run. He was a passionate advocate of markets at a time, the end of the eighteenth century, when market organization of the whole economy was a rather new and radical idea. Vestiges of feudal obligations and commitments and the hold of old traditions continued to severely limit what people thought of doing or were allowed to do. In this sense, Smith was a revolutionary. He wanted to see a speedy end to vestiges of feudalism, and he wanted to see society reorganized on market principles that would allow people the freedom to defy encumbrances of feudal tradition. For Smith, the entire society was better off when people were able to discover their real talents and move about in search of places to put them to use. This had a strongly religious overtone, and Smith thought that misapplication of talent was both shameful and wasteful. He understood a market as a mechanism that enables talent and resources to go where they are most needed. In this sense, true markets constitute an assault on traditional ties and commitments.[1]

Within a few years of publication of *The Wealth of Nations*, the British economist David Ricardo helped explain more clearly why everyone can, in theory, be better off if markets are operating smoothly. Ricardo's explanation was based on the concept of "comparative advantage." If talented people who can do many things very well have an incentive to focus their effort on what others cannot do, rather than spending some of their time on things others have the capacity to do, the whole world will be better off. Ricardo also thought about national economies in terms of comparative advantage. His view was that some countries might have advantages in manufacturing and others in agriculture, and that free trade and open markets would allow each type of country to grow richer by exploiting its natural advantages and importing everything else. Advocates of globalization are still saying essentially the same thing. Market theory sounds like it makes a lot of sense, at least if markets are perfect and have all the qualities Smith and Ricardo talked about. A *very* important point to remember, however, is that markets are human creations and are never perfect. Thus they won't always generate the rosy consequences Smith and Ricardo envisioned. Sociologists have a lot to say about this, and when we do we are contributing to a better understanding of the economy.[2]

It is worthwhile stopping to remember that markets are one form of organization, but not the only form. The former Soviet Union, for example, had a "command and control" economy based on *hierarchy*, with centralized planning and decision making. Communist economies ran for decades, guided by the hierarchical command and control of a government that defined what society "needed most," rather than by the "invisible hand of market" incentives enticing people to do what is in most demand. The Communist economies did run; they just did not run very well. A social scientist might ask: How are the economies of different societies organized differently (which calls for description)? Why are they organized differently (which calls for explanation of causes)? With what outcomes (which calls for better understanding of consequences)? How does change come about and why does it take so long (which calls for capturing causal dynamics in the form of predictive principles)? How can we improve policy (which calls for applying our principles to social engineering)? All these questions are sociological questions, as much or even more than economic ones. At their root, they force recognition that there are different ways of organizing interaction among a plethora of people. This requires that we set our sights on understanding why one form (markets, or hierarchies, or networks) prevails at a given place and time and over a given range of activity.³

THE BEGINNINGS OF SOCIOLOGY IN BRITAIN

Adam Smith's work signaled a serious beginning of social scientific study of the economy. Intellectually emboldened by Smith (in Scotland), and empowered by Comte (in France) with his optimism about the prospects for social science, Harriet Martineau and others in Britain took up the task of engaging in pioneering sociological research, as described in the last chapter. Eighteen years younger than Martineau was another great English sociologist, Herbert Spencer (1820–1902). Although Spencer did not have a university position (indeed, he had been sickly as a boy and was almost entirely homeschooled), he was a great intellect with an enormous public following. For example, Spencer's concept of "survival of the fittest" was useful to Charles Darwin as Darwin refined his theory of evolution.⁴ Darwin's principle of evolution has sociological applications. We know, for example, that when organizations are divided into different units that remain somewhat separate from each other, such as academic departments in a university, those units sometimes develop their own, distinct cultures.

Principle of Evolution: *Other things being equal, the smaller subpopulations are and the less contact they have with each other, the more rapidly and more dramatically they will differentiate from each other.*

This simple insight is crucial for our understanding of contemporary human civilization. Trade and globalization and electronic communication all reduce isolation, and by doing so they challenge social heterogeneity and reduce cultural distinctiveness. The concept of societal evolution has occupied a pronounced place in Herbert Spencer's sociology.

Unlike Martineau, Spencer was more heavily influenced by Smith than Comte, and this is clearly evident in the approach Spencer developed to sociology. Above all else, Spencer shared Smith's faith in the "invisible hand of the market." Drawing from Smith, Spencer recognized markets as the mechanism that would make people break down the doors of isolation. Different people and practices would then be in direct competition with one another. In theory, the most desirable and efficient practices would be copied far and wide, and people would come to recognize that many of their idiosyncratic practices were failed experiments that should be replaced by more adaptive strategies. Some readers will applaud this view. Others will be repelled by it. But whether cultural pluralism is better or worse than homogenization is not the issue in this chapter. The issue is the premise that market dynamics, by bringing people into closer contact, have made the world more homogeneous rather than more heterogeneous.

Throughout Spencer's sociology, there is a clear recognition of markets as an organizational form worth studying. Whatever the limits of utilitarian economics and the various intellectual frameworks it helps inspire, the notion that incentives influence supply is an important insight that should be in our repertoire of predictive principles.

Principle of Supply and Demand: *Other things being equal, the more scarce something is, and the more sought after it is, then the more costly it becomes, the more incentive potential producers have to enter into production of it, and the more incentive consumers have to look for substitutes for it.*

Smith and other economists working in the utilitarian economics tradition recognized that price is subject to fluctuation, partly as a function of supply and demand. When people are free to make exchange decisions, how much consumers will be called on to pay for something is a positive function of how many people want it and how badly they want it, and a negative function of how much is available from suppliers right now. But as price changes, so do incentives for new suppliers to begin supplying, for old suppliers to increase supply, and for current and future consumers/users to find suitable alternatives.

ECONOMISTS SWITCHING TO SOCIOLOGY

German economist Karl Marx and German economist-turned-sociologist Max Weber were two of the key founders of the sociological tradition. Their work is the topic of the next two chapters. But many other economists were also pioneers of the intellectual frontier between sociology and economics. Two of these, Thorstein Veblen in the United States and Vilfredo Pareto in Switzerland, made extremely important contributions to the development of sociology. In his famous 1899 book, *The Theory of the Leisure Class*, Veblen observed that people sometimes use market resources to elevate their social standing through "conspicuous consumption." That is, people seek to *appear to others* as smart, hard working, and having good taste, not just by demonstrating those qualities directly, but by living in big houses, wearing the right clothes, eating trendy food, and going on long vacations to far-away places.[5]

Conspicuous consumption is a very powerful idea in itself. But if we look beyond the surface we find that Veblen's concept speaks to the very character of economics and sociology as disciplines. Veblen introduced conspicuous consumption as evidence that people are driven primarily by a desire to acquire status, rather than by calculations about material gain per se. For example, many business people are driven to make more money not because they need the money or even want the money for itself, but because accumulating more money is a measure of stature and success in the circles in which they travel.

Once one accepts the premise that desire for status is what really drives rational choice calculations, sociology becomes indispensable for proper economic analysis, because it is sociology, more than economics, that addresses the question, Why on earth do people value what they do? If Veblen was right, sociology subsumes economics in this crucial respect. Simply stated, standard utilitarian economics presents far more questions than it answers. Certainly, it is worthwhile saying that, "if given a choice, people will act in ways designed to get what they want" and "if people have good information they will make wise decisions." But explaining why people value what they do is left to sociology.

Over the years, many famous economists have embraced sociology because they believed that economics as it is commonly practiced leaves out too many pieces of the puzzle. Perhaps the most important of these was Vilfredo Pareto, who oriented sociology toward explaining major economic trends. His ideas are perhaps most succinctly captured in a collection of papers published in 1923, *The Transformation of Democracy,* which explores recurring patterns of socioeconomic and political history. People get swept up in speculative bubbles during periods of rapid and sustained economic growth. They see everyone else making easy profits, with little apparent risk. As that happens, people begin to want more for themselves. Caution is thrown to the wind and people begin acting imprudently, paying insufficient attention to possible costs and exposure to risk. Of course, Pareto did not think everyone would be swept up by the spirit of the times in equal degree. But aggregate trends do make a difference. Some periods are characterized by higher levels of desire for pursuit of pleasure and immediate gratification, and by reduced levels of caution, lower savings rates, and more cavalier attitudes about risk. Those social trends encourage speculative investment and consumer exuberance. This accelerates short-term economic growth, but undermines the prospects for longer-term economic well-being at the societal level.

When the cumulative consequences of exuberant consumer spending and speculative investment begin to accumulate and manifest themselves, an economic downturn is inevitable. Bad economic times make people more cautious, show a higher propensity to save, begin to ridicule comfort and pleasure seeking, and demonstrate aversion to risk when making decisions. Vilfredo Pareto was one of the most famous economists of all time, the "father of mathematical economics." And yet he left economics for sociology because he was convinced that the key to understanding what happens in the economy was in developing social science principles explaining shifts in public sentiment and mood.[6]

Over the longer term, savings accumulate because people try to put something away for a rainy day. However, people eventually grow tired of the social constraint imposed by the more conservative climate, and the cycle renews itself when consumers start spending more. In this way, Pareto offers a cyclical analysis involving a clear interplay between social, economic, and political trends. Following a long period of tight social constraint, initial efforts to deregulate and ease up on enforcement of rules almost always produce economic benefits. Visible benefits add momentum to the trend toward deregulation and relaxation of enforcement of remaining rules. But as trends toward liberalization and deregulation gain more momentum, there is a tendency to "overshoot." That is, the trend carries so far in one direction that negative consequences begin to accumulate.

Trends are rarely reversed until significant negative consequences have accumulated. The more confining rules are and the longer the period over which confining rules are strictly enforced, the greater the number of people who will come to favor relaxation of rules, launching a long-term trend toward hedonistic and speculative behavior of all kinds. The more relaxed and sporadically enforced rules are, the greater the number of people who will perceive themselves to be harmed because of a lack of rules/enforcement, launching a long-term trend toward greater social constraint that restricts freedom and discourages experimentation of all kinds. These observations leave too many unanswered questions to merit being called true explanatory principles, but they do help to illuminate sociological phenomena that influence the flow of economic events and cry out for more study.

MARKETS VERSUS HIERARCHIES
VERSUS NETWORKS

Sociologists necessarily concern themselves with markets as an important mode of organization. But there are other important forms of organization. These include hierarchies, as pointed out by Oliver Williamson in his conceptually important 1975 book, *Markets and Hierarchies*,[7] and networks, as explored in the Manuel Castells's 1996 book, *The Rise of the Network Society*.[8]

An illustration may help. Market organization implies that the partners with whom one cooperates are easily changed. If I don't like the brand of yogurt sold at the store where I normally shop, I can easily visit one of the other grocery stores in my neighborhood. No law or social custom or alliance restricts where I shop. For me, deciding where to shop and what to buy is a market decision. Where can I get what I want at the best price and most convenient location today? My situation is very different from the situation of my father when he was my age. My father did the grocery shopping and a friendship tie dictated where he shopped. Like so many small-town people, or in his case a small-town migrant to a big city, he did not allow himself the freedom of a market decision about where to shop. The decision was made by a deep bond of friendship. We shopped at the small store of "Johnny the butcher," who had far less variety and higher prices than the competition because he had a very small shop. But for us, where to shop was a matter of friendship and social commitment. This was not a decision involving any economic calculation. It was not a market matter. The economics were irrelevant. This kind of experience remains common in small towns, in the "urban villages" at the heart of America's cities, and in many ethnic enclaves. For some people, shopping activity is organized within market structures, but for other people it is organized within network structures.

Sometimes, hierarchy also looks like a market. When I lived in Alabama, there was state "liquor control." That means there was only one legal place in my town of twenty thousand people to buy wine or beer. My choices were to buy alcohol at that state-controlled liquor store or not buy at all. That was hierarchy at work. It was by no means a true market. It was not necessarily a bad system. But whatever it was, the sale of alcohol was not organized on true market principles. Had it been, privately owned liquor stores would have opened and there would have been much more choice.

The broad implications of this subject become apparent if we think about corporate decisions. General Motors has the resources to produce all of the car batteries it needs for the cars it sells. But GM can purchase batteries cheaper than it can manufacture them. Weighing all the short- and long-term costs involved, what should GM do? This is an exceedingly important sociological question, because it goes directly to the heart of the question of alternative modes of social organization. Is it best to follow a market mode of organization and save money by purchasing batteries on the market? Or would it be better to adopt hierarchy as the mode of organization and produce batteries inside the company? Or might a third strategy, the network strategy, be preferable? A network strategy would suggest a strategic alliance with GM turning to an outside vendor but promising a long-term (or at least intermediate-term) commitment with a supplier promising to meet needs and to innovate as necessary.

In a very important 1937 paper, economist Ronald Coase explained that risk presented by uncertainty is a critical factor when selecting among alternative modes of organization.[9] If one battery is not at the right place at the right time, a $20,000 car has to be pushed into a parking lot instead of driven onto a showroom floor. And if the undelivered part is a transmission gear rather than a battery, an entire production line will grind to a halt. So the relative risk and potential costs associated with different uncertainties have to be figured into business calculations. The greater the threat posed by the possibility of labor unrest or other uncertainties that could disrupt supply, the smarter it is to avoid what looks like cost-saving market solutions that, in fact, increase exposure to risk. In other words, uncertainty tends to make otherwise unattractive hierarchical/bureaucratic organizational solutions look better than they would otherwise appear, and tends to make otherwise attractive market solutions for organizing activity less attractive than they would otherwise appear. This insight won Coase a Nobel Prize for economics, but is perhaps more important in sociological than in economic analysis, because sociologists almost always treat form of organization as something that is potentially variable and must be explained.

Uncertainty Principle of Hierarchy: *Other things being equal, the greater the risk of uncertainty implicit in market solutions, the more cost-effective market solutions need to be in order to make them rational in comparison with hierarchy as a mode of organization.*

Many factors need to be considered when one is weighing risk. Labor unrest and quality of component parts are two of the factors most people instinctively recognize as important, although there are many others. Sociological analyses often deal with risk factors.

Implications of improved technology also weigh heavily in sociological analysis. At first glance, most improvements in transportation and communication technology favor market organization over hierarchical organization, as do improvements in manufacturing precision and equipment reliability. But the connection between these factors is actually quite complicated. Technological advancement and the scientific knowledge explosion tend to force organizations to maintain a steady stream of innovation in order to remain competitive. When customization and innovation are required, sustained network partnerships tend to be superior to either markets or hierarchies, because they provide more flexibility than hierarchies and generate more sustained commitment than markets. Networking tends to optimize the balance between (a) the need for long-term commitments justifying the cost of innovation and (b) the need for flexibility required to be successful at innovation.

Innovation/Complexity Principle of Networking: *Other things being equal, the advisability of network/strategic alliance solutions to organizational challenges is a positive function of the complexity of activity and the necessity to maintain ongoing creativity and innovation in order to remain competitive.*

The way sociologists have borrowed from and built on the utilitarian economics tradition sharpens social scientists' conceptual understanding of contemporary challenges and adds to their toolbox of explanatory insights.

RECAP

The utilitarian economic tradition is an exceedingly important part of sociology's heritage, because market mechanisms are one of the main organizing strategies human beings use to coordinate interaction. But hierarchies and networks are also important organizational strategies. Uncertainty tends to privilege hierarchies over markets and networks, and need for innovation tends to privilege networks over markets and hierarchies. When markets prevail, rational calculation is just as likely to be aimed at maximizing social status or nonrational tastes as material well-being. Market solutions do tend to limit sociocultural diversity, which declines as isolated populations increase in size and come into closer contact. These insights make up an important part of sociology's intellectual tradition.

NOTES

1. Adam Smith, *The Wealth of Nations* (1776; reprint, New York: Irwin, 1963).
2. Charles Powers, "Bridging the Conceptual Gap between Economics and Sociology," *Journal of Socio-Economics* 25, no. 2 (June 1996): 225–43.
3. Jerald Hage and Charles Powers, *Post-Industrial Lives* (Thousand Oaks, Calif.: Sage, 1992).
4. Herbert Spencer, *Herbert Spencer: Structure, Function, and Evolution*, edited by Stanislav Andreski (London: Michael Joseph, 1971).
5. Thorstein Veblen, *The Theory of the Leisure Class* (1899; reprint, New York: New American Library, 1953).
6. Vilfredo Pareto, *The Transformation of Democracy* (New Brunswick, N.J.: Transaction, 1984).
7. Oliver Williamson, *Markets and Hierarchies* (New York: Free Press, 1975).
8. Manuel Castells, *The Rise of the Network Society* (Malden, Mass.: Blackwell, 1996).
9. Ronald Coase, "The Nature of the Firm," *Economica*, no. 4 (November 1937): 386–405.

SOME TERMS TO KNOW

Transparency. The ready availability of complete and accurate information.

Conspicuous Consumption. Seeking to enhance one's own prestige by spending money in ways that send visible signals that suggest that an individual should be regarded as a person of merit.

Overshoot. The tendency for the momentum of social trends to continue in the same direction until mounting problems make additional movement in that direction untenable.

REVIEW OF PRINCIPLES

Principle of Evolution: *Other things being equal, the smaller subpopulations are and the less contact they have with each other, the more rapidly and more dramatically they will differentiate from each other.*

Principle of Supply and Demand: *Other things being equal, the more scarce something is, and the more sought after it is, then the more costly it becomes, the more incentive potential producers have to enter into production of it, and the more incentive consumers have to look for substitutes for it.*

Uncertainty Principle of Hierarchy: *Other things being equal, the greater the risk of uncertainty implicit in market solutions, the more cost-effective market solutions need to be in order to make them rational in comparison with hierarchy as a mode of organization.*

Innovation/Complexity Principle of Networking: *Other things being equal, the advisability of network/strategic alliance solutions to organizational challenges is a positive function of the complexity of activity and the necessity to maintain ongoing creativity and innovation in order to remain competitive.*

CHAPTER REVIEW TEST

Check your answers in the back of the book. If you get any wrong, reread chapter 6 and try to get comfortable with the themes of the chapter before moving on to chapter 7.

1. What are the characteristics of a perfect market?

2. What is the Principle of Evolution and what does it suggest about globalization?

3. When is hierarchy preferable to market organization?

APPLICATION EXERCISE

Make a list of things college students might weigh when they select a major. These could include many things, such as perceptions about simple enjoyment of the subject matter, employability, earning power, potential for helping others, and opportunity for adventure. They might also include course load, how hard the grading is in different fields, and opportunities for meeting members of the opposite sex. Or perhaps the important concerns are not listed here. In your view, what concerns tend to be most important for the majority of college students?

Ask yourself why you think different people set the priorities they do. That is, why do people value what they value and why do they want what they want? Does identity enter into this picture? Do roles? Do patterns of inequality? For whom? Why? How can we make sense of all this? Is sociological insight about people's motives and priorities necessary to make sense of their decisions?

KARL MARX AND THE ORGANIZATION OF RESISTANCE FROM BELOW

Recognizing the Opposing Interests of Different Groups

People in the mid-nineteenth century were well aware that the world was being transformed by the juggernaut of European industrial capitalism. At that time, the heart of this industrial juggernaut stretched along the River Rhine from Germany into Holland, down the coast and slightly in-land to Paris, across the English Channel to London, and finally up to the mill towns of northern England. That was the industrial center of the world. It is actually a very small geographic area with a history of trade and contact among the lowland Germans, Dutch, English, and people of the northeast of France. Technological innovation and new commercial ideas always diffused quickly among localities in this region, a fact that turns out to be an important element in European commercial history.

THE LABOR THEORY OF VALUE

Karl Marx (1818–1883) was a part of this scene, having been born and raised in Tier in the western part of Germany. Marx went to Berlin during his university years and was influenced by ideas of the recently deceased philosopher Georg Friedrich Hegel (Germany, 1770–1831). Hegel was a leading philosopher in Germany when Marx was young. Hegel advanced the thought-provoking notion that ideas progress through the dialectical clash of opposites. In Hegel's terms, thesis meets antithesis and gives rise to a new synthesis.

Marx always considered himself an economist, but he was not like the utilitarian economists described in the last chapter. Marx was a "radical economist" who employed a "labor theory of value." For Marx, and indeed for anyone believing in a labor theory of value, the worth of something depends on how much effort goes into producing and delivering it. From this point of view, a handmade piece of furniture that was laboriously but awkwardly crafted (OK, like the ones I have made) should be worth more than a piece of well-milled but mass-produced furniture that is turned out quickly by a machine.

The labor theory of value has some problems. Although some hand-crafted furniture is both functional and exquisite, some is neither. And although some machine-made pieces of furniture are ugly and impractical, other pieces are extremely functional and quite attractive. For most people, value is a function of more than the amount of time and effort that goes into making something available. There are issues of quality and functional design, of aesthetics, and of simply being in the right place at the right time. The labor theory of value tends to miss all this. But the labor theory of value does help us to see things we might otherwise overlook. Who actually performs the work that makes industrial wealth possible? Do those people get what they deserve? If not, how does the distribution of rewards really work? Marx looked at the value corporations produce and decided that capitalists, who were in control of the distribution of rewards, took more of the value being produced than their efforts really warranted, and left workers with less of the value being produced than they really deserved. The difference between the value produced by workers and the wages returned to those workers is a "surplus" in value that those workers create but never see. The extraction of that surplus value from businesses and into the pockets of owners is at the heart of what Marx described as the system of capitalist exploitation.

This view led Marx to conceive of class in a way that is qualitatively distinct from the understanding most people have of the term. For most people, "class" has come to mean economic well-being. A person with more money is higher class than a person with less money. Marx's concept of class was different. His concept of class was defined in terms of *social relationship to means of production*. Marx believed that people who lived by selling their labor for wages had interests in common (class interests) with all other wage earners (all other people whose social relation to the production process was that they became "wage slaves" by selling their own labor in exchange for wages to live on). Correspondingly, all people who lived by purchasing and directing the labor of others (all capitalists) shared things in common.

Marx believed that recognition of true class interests could be elusive. As long as owners of means of production also tend to control government and news media, many wage earners are likely to be convinced that the "right" policies and programs are actually those policies and programs that benefit owners in a number of ways, including allowing owners to continue extracting "surplus value" form wage earners. Marx felt that people had a tendency to speak and work against their own interests because of a failure to accurately understand what their own interests really were. He called this "false consciousness," in contrast with truly accurate "class consciousness."

The labor theory of value does not assign much credit to entrepreneurial initiative or marketing genius. Many people reject Marxian economics at its intellectual core because Marx's analysis of capitalism is built on a labor theory of value. But even if we disagree with the labor theory of value, it is important to understand it in order to appreciate how Marx arrived at the revealing insights about conflict for which he is remembered by sociologists. Yet, before leaping to Marx's sociology of conflict, it is important to set the stage by reviewing more of his economics.

DIALECTICAL THEORY

While a young adult in Berlin, Marx was a rabble-rouser and caught the attention of the Prussian secret police for his radical, pro-worker, anti-imperialist views. That meant having to leave. Although Germany was not yet unified into a single country (unification occurred three decades later, after the Franco–Prussian War) Prussia was the strongest of the German states and the Prussian secret police operated throughout the entirety of what would become Germany. This made staying anywhere in the future Germany unsafe for Marx, so he went to Paris, where he was a vocal advocate of radical political change. When Marx's fiery presence overstayed its welcome in France, he took it to England, which had a somewhat more tolerant intellectual climate.

England was a very good place for Marx to continue to study and write.

Not only was England the seedbed of industrial capitalism, but Marx's close friend and collaborator, Friedrich Engels (1820–1895), was a member of a wealthy family who owned textile factories there. Living in England put Marx in the position where Engels could open doors for him. Marx and Engels even distributed one of the first mass surveys in history, when they passed out questionnaires to thousands of British factory workers (although they got a low response rate).

The ties Engels had to community-minded young factory workers were invaluable. Accounts have it that Mary Burns and others acquainted with Engels first showed Engels, and then later Marx, what was happening to wage earners as the industrial revolution took hold. Engels and Marx thus acquired insight informed by the daily experiences of some members of England's industrial working class. Engels's own writing about the English factory system, especially his 1844 book, *The Origin of the Family, Private Property, and the State,* was seminal.[1] Although Engels is best remembered as the longtime friend and collaborator (coauthor) of Karl Marx, it is likely that some of the ideas people associate with Marx were actually brought to the collaboration by Engels, who was a formidable intellect in his own right.

Despite the importance of Engels and others, Karl Marx was recognized as the most towering intellect among the radicals who indicted the system of power and privilege of nineteenth-century capitalism. As an economist of the mid-nineteenth century, Marx understood economics in substantial measure based on his reading of Adam Smith and David Ricardo, but his understanding also incorporated the labor theory of value. To his study of the economic situation of his times, Marx also imported a Hegelian view that processes of change revolve around a thesis, confronted by some antithesis, leading to a new synthesis. Thus, instead of viewing economic change in cyclical terms, as Pareto would, Marx came to view economic history in dialectical terms. This means he focused on the way an economic epoch, such as feudalism, can "sow the seeds of its own destruction," giving rise to an entirely new economic system, like capitalism. In turn, Marx predicted that capitalism would undo itself by "sowing the seeds of its own destruction."

THE MEANING OF CLASS

Marx, ever the economist, maintained strict adherence to economic determinism. He was firmly convinced that systems of ideas (e.g., religion) and everything else of seeming importance about society (e.g., form of government) were really shaped by the social relations of production in a particular economic system, such as the wage-labor production system in a capitalist society. In keeping with this approach, Marx defined economic classes in terms of position within a system of social relations of production. In capitalism, the social relations of production revolve around who was hiring whom. In capitalism, therefore, Marx would have said the main classes were made up of wage earners (proletarians) and those who purchased and directed the labor of others (capitalists). Marx was convinced that one's class, defined in this way, was the single most important factor influencing everything else about experience, opportunity, and quality of life. In capitalism, the wage labor system ties together people who survive by selling their labor (that is, a proletariat class made up of "wage-slave" workers) and people who live by purchasing and directing the labor of others (a capitalist class). By paying laborers less than the value they actually produce through their labor, capitalists live as "parasites" on the "surplus value" workers create but do not have distributed to them.

THE LAWS OF CAPITALISM

As an economist, Marx is primarily remembered for his analysis of the "laws" ordaining capitalism's growth and eventual collapse. Marx introduced his laws of capitalism in *Capital*,[2] the first volume of which was released in 1867, and they are very neatly summarized in a 1978 paper by Richard Appelbaum.[3] Marx's law of accumulation of capital ordained the growth of capitalist market economies. Based on his readings of Smith, Marx was convinced that the market freedoms and productive capacity of industrial capitalism marked a qualitative advance beyond the socially restrictive nature and lack of material productivity of feudal societies. That is why Marx believed that capitalism presented the possibility of material abundance for all. By freeing people to follow the profit incentive, capitalism directs innovative talent toward the satisfaction of needs and wants. The natural result is "capital accumulation" (the law of accumulation of capital in a society). Everyone strives to copy and improve upon the success of others. Profits are reinvested in more machines in order to further expand productive capacity. Still following Smith, Marx believed that competition among producers would encourage cost-saving innovation and price restraint. In general, this would make life better for people, at least over the short term during the early stages of capitalism. The amount of physical capital (machines) and social capital (wage labor employment arrangements) would grow over time, hence, "capital accumulation."

But Marx predicted that competing capitalists would eventually experience long periods of "falling rate of profit" in the battle for market share, especially during bouts of technology-driven overproduction. Less-profitable companies would be absorbed by more-profitable competitors. As a result, productive capacity would become increasingly concentrated, ending with exploitation of workers and consumers at the hands of monopolies. This was the operation of Marx's "law of centralization of capital."

Centralization, Marx predicted, would fuel a trend toward more extreme class division. That is, the rich would grow even richer, the poor would grow even poorer, and very importantly, the middle class would shrink rather than grow, as middle-class people (that is, the self-employed) either would become successful capitalists (by hiring employees) or join the ranks of wage labor (by accepting jobs). From this point of view, doctors who give up private practice and go to work for a health maintenance organization (HMO) are joining the working class. They may not think of themselves as proletarians (because "false consciousness" can blind people to their true class interests), but Marx would have argued that those doctors are progressively being transformed from small-scale capitalists (if they used to have employees) into wage-earning working people.

With the progression of time, Marx predicted that workers would lose decision-making authority over the work process as a result of the "deskilling" of their jobs. Deskilling occurs as machines are introduced and expensive skilled workers are replaced with less-expensive unskilled workers. Furthermore, workers would become alienated from their work, alienated from other people, and in a sense even alienated from themselves. Marx felt that this combination of factors would necessarily produce economic desperation and extreme class antagonisms leading to some kind of revolution. Capitalism would, in effect, "sow the seeds of its own destruction." Thus, in *Capital*, Marx put a lot of additional analytical detail into the basic model of change outlined some twenty years earlier by Marx and Engels when they wrote *The Communist Manifesto*.[4]

MARX'S CONTRIBUTION TO SOCIOLOGY

Although Marx's economics was based on a labor theory of value that most people reject, his work produced a principle of social conflict that is very insightful and has withstood the test of time. The bigger and more consistent the gap between the "haves" and "have nots," the harder it is to ignore that gap or explain it away. Marx's insights can be communicated in a principle that we can reasonably call the Principle of Intergroup Antagonism.

Principle of Intergroup Antagonism: *Other things being equal, the greater the level of inequality between groups, the greater the homogeneity within groups, the more substantial the barriers to mobility between groups, and the greater the level of intergroup competition over scarce resources, then the more likely members of both groups are to have a sense of distinct identity and the more profound intergroup antagonisms will be.*

This principle exemplifies good theory. It offers significant insight about the way the world operates. And it does so in sufficiently clear yet generic terms that the implications the principle has for a wide range of situations is clear. This is a principle that enables us to make predictions about things it is important that we not ignore.

RECAP

Importantly, the cumulative body of sociological evidence suggests that Marx's Principle of Intergroup Antagonism is correct, at least in its broad contours. What failed was Marx's economics, which led him to incorrectly predict the demise of the middle class. Marx, a self-identified economist, was actually not a world-class economist because his analysis is predicated on a labor theory of value, which has many problems. But Marx, who never saw himself as a sociologist, can be considered a world-class sociologist for developing a predictive principle informing our understanding of something truly significant: intergroup antagonism. By unlocking important mysteries of intergroup conflict, Marx added significantly to the foundation for a social scientific understanding of society.

He gave us a window for beginning to understand organized resistance, from below, against a society's ruling elite. This also helps us to appreciate certain types of group division, such as racial/ethnic conflict.

NOTES

1. Friedrich Engels, *The Origin of the Family, Private Property, and the State* (1844; reprint, New York: International, 1972).
2. Karl Marx, *Capital* (1867; reprint, New York: International Publishers, 1967).
3. Richard Appelbaum, "Marx's Theory of the Falling Rate of Profit: Toward a Dialectical Analysis of Structural Social Change," *American Sociological Review* 43, no. 1 (February 1978): 67–80.
4. Karl Marx and Friedrich Engels, *The Communist Manifesto* (1848; reprint, Northbrook, Ill.: AMH, 1955).

SOME TERMS TO KNOW

Surplus Value. Wealth initially created through the effort of wage earners but diverted into the pockets of business owners.

Class. Position within the system of social relationships around which the production process is organized.

False Consciousness. Failure to recognize one's own class interests, to the point of supporting continuation of policies and programs that actually work to the detriment of one's own interests.

PRINCIPLE REVIEW

Principle of Intergroup Antagonism: *Other things being equal, the greater the level of inequality between groups, the greater the homogeneity within groups, the more substantial the barriers to mobility between groups, and the greater the level of intergroup competition over scarce resources, then the more likely members of both groups are to have a sense of distinct identity and the more profound intergroup antagonisms will be.*

CHAPTER REVIEW TEST

Check your answers in the back of the book. If you get any wrong, reread chapter 7, thinking about it as you go, before moving on to chapter 8.

1. What is Marx's Principle of Intergroup Antagonism?

2. Was Marx a cyclical theorist or a dialectical theorist? How does cyclical theory differ from dialectical theory?

3. How did Marx define class?

APPLICATION EXERCISE

American labor history has been characterized by much racial/ethnic division. That is, workers from one ancestral homeland often feel they are locked in competition for jobs with workers of other ancestries. Deep and lasting antagonisms sometimes develop. How do you think Marx would analyze this? Do you think he would feel the Principle of Intergroup Antagonism was validated or challenged? How do you think he would apply his concepts of "class consciousness" and "false consciousness"?

8

MAX WEBER AND THE PRIMACY OF VALUES

Moving Past Economic Determinism

Max Weber (Germany, 1864–1920) is one of the "gang of four" theorists most sociologists regard as having provided the intellectual cornerstones of the discipline. In comparison with the others in the "gang of four" (Durkheim, Marx, and Mead), Weber's legacy is somewhat harder to summarize. Nevertheless, he is a particularly important figure in the history of sociology.

HISTORICAL ECONOMICS IN THE BACKGROUND

Weber began his working life as an economics professor. He was a young but respected member of Germany's "historical school of economics." The historical school dominated economics departments in German universities during the late nineteenth century and differed significantly from the utilitarian economics dominating in Britain and the United States. The story of competing schools of economics is worth a little attention, because it helps us better understand Max Weber and equips us to help recognize some important "founder effects" that continue to have (sometimes underappreciated) impact on contemporary sociology.

What distinguished German historical economics from British utilitarian economics was a conviction among historical economists that: (a) each economy is unique in some way, (b) economists should *look to the particulars of religious and cultural history to discover values that drive the differences*

97

between economies, and (c) economists should look to the *particulars of legal codes, banking systems, and other organizational forms to identify national differences in institutional environments and mechanisms that keep economies distinct.* An appreciation for the importance of religion and other aspects of culture, and sensitivity to the institutional distinctiveness of each society, differentiated German historical economics, which the young Max Weber was a part of, from mainstream British utilitarian economics. In this respect, Weber was very much like Thorstein Veblen, who himself was influenced by the German historical economists, and Vilfredo Pareto, who shared historical economic interest in belief systems, even though exasperated with the historical economists because they were so infatuated with the idea of historical uniqueness that they had difficulty arriving at useful theoretical generalizations. The point is that, like Pareto and Veblen, Weber was acutely interested in values. And like Pareto and Veblen, Weber understood that an economy does not function in a sociological vacuum.

Historical economics also differs from the "radical economics" of Karl Marx. Radical economists tended to see the world as divided between exploiters and the exploited, each having diametrically opposed interests. This led radical economists to see the world as neatly divided between (poor) "good guys" and (rich) "bad guys." Historical economists, by contrast, viewed each national economy as separate from other national economies and presumed that each economic class within a particular country had its fate tied to every other class in that same country. The historical economists believed that the common interests of all classes in one country formed a natural basis of solidarity linking the different classes of that country together. So their use of the term *solidarity* closely parallels use of the term in the contemporary parlance of European Christians, and even that of the Solidarity movement in Poland, which helped bring an end to the Soviet era, but is quite different from "solidarity" as the term is employed by Marxists.

It is an interesting historical fact that self-consciously Catholic and Christian approaches to the study of economics, a "social economics" perspective, emerged out of the German school of historical economics that Weber was a part of. Social economists have spent the last century calling on privileged people to support living wage and other provisions for the benefit of working people. And why? Not out of pity. Their support comes from a kind of "solidarity," or an awareness that the fate of capitalists is interconnected with the fate of workers.[1] Marxist scholars would think of this as "false consciousness." False or not, it is certainly a different consciousness than the Marxists possess. "Solidarism" is based on recognition of the ways in which the interests of different economic classes are intertwined rather than in total conflict. Supporting "living wage" and other policies is a way of strengthening the whole society by supporting labor. It is seen, from this perspective, as in everyone's interest. Likewise, expecting everyone to come to work on time, work hard, work carefully, and work conscientiously is a way of strengthening the whole society by supporting capital.

Historical economics was in a state of intellectual crisis in Weber's time. German historical economists were ever aware of the complexity of the social world, and consequently hesitant to engage in analytical simplification, thus the development of theory in German historical economics floundered. This had a very heavy impact on Weber, who was strained quite literally to a breaking point by the challenge of trying to develop a science of society informed by both his historical economic training and his rising sociological sensibilities. Frustrated with the slow pace of theoretical progress being made by historical economists and troubled by his own personal and family problems, including unresolved conflicts with his father, Weber had a breakdown. As he began recovery, he also began writing, first with an attack on the vacuous state of theory in the German historical economic tradition, and then with a trailblazing set of books setting out methods, conceptual tools, and an analytical framework contributing to the new and promising science of sociology.

ANALYTICAL ABSTRACTION FOLLOWING THE IDEAL-TYPE METHOD

Max Weber's intellectual interests were broad. Even eighty years after his death, Weber remains among the most widely read sociologists, because he touched on so many issues with such penetrating insight. But for that very same reason, Weber's ideas defy easy summary. His strength was in being extremely insightful about many different things. And as a workaholic without children, he was incredibly prolific and left an immense body of writing as a legacy sociologists continue to mine for bits of revelation. An excellent collection of excerpts (drawn from various Weber publications between 1906 and 1924, is available in *From Max Weber*, edited by Hans Gerth and C. Wright Mills.[2]

Weber's impact can be best appreciated if we remember that he was interested in creating systems of analytical categories that would simplify the challenge of performing social science investigation by highlighting the most crucial ways in which one social setting can vary from other similar settings. In doing so, Weber often sought to use what he called "ideal-types" to categorize the major forms that particular kinds of phenomena can assume. An example is *authority*. Sociologists define authority as the *legitimate right to make certain kinds of decisions and expect those decisions to be carried out without having to resort to coercion.* Gaining compliance through the use or threat of coercive force is an exercise in raw power, putting it outside the scope of Weber's definition of authority. Weber looked around at all the different systems of authority he was familiar with, through reading as well as through experience, and realized that they clump together in three different types. Those major categories constituted a set of ideal-type categories.

Authority is an important sociological concept and deserves an illustration. At most colleges, professors have the authority (the legitimate right to make decisions of a particular kind) to decide (within very broad limits constrained only a tad by community standards) what students should read in conjunction with a class. But college professors typically do not have the authority to order students to wash the professor's car or mow the professor's lawn as a condition of succeeding in a class. Stop to think of it. Assigning students to read class-relevant material is legitimate for a professor, and assigning students to wash cars or mow lawns is not. Some professor somewhere may try to issue the order to "wash my car," and might even succeed in gaining compliance with that order. But such an order would not be legitimate at an American college, and compliance would be in response to something other than professional "authority" in the pure sociological sense of the term. The student could be an employee at a local car wash and acting in her role as car wash employee (not her role as student). Or the faculty member could be ill and the student could be performing an act of compassion (in a role as a community volunteer). Perhaps the student could be a daughter of the professor (responding in her role as daughter rather than in the student role). Or perhaps the student could simply be responding to coercive force, which would make this an instance of raw exercise of power rather than legitimate authority as Weber defined it. Instances such as these tended to reinforce Weber's conviction that we need a system of conceptual definitions, and that typologies can serve as tools to help us see what is real and pertinent when we study sociological subject matter.

In looking at concepts such as authority, Weber believed that construction of ideal-types would assist sociologists in arriving at a better conceptual understanding of societal phenomena. An ideal-type is just a listing of common forms (different types of something), or of distinguishing characteristics (features common to a type of phenomenon). Political authority, for example, is present in some form in all societies, but just because all societies can be said to have a system of political authority does not mean that the system of authority is the same in every society. Constructing an "ideal type" forces us to think clearly about *salient distinctions* that might be worth focusing on.

Importantly, Weber recognized that identifying common forms was not the same as identifying perfect forms or best forms or most desirable forms. "Ideal-types" are ideal in the sense of capturing meaningful essence, and nothing more. They are not ideal in the sense of being "best" forms or "ultimate" goals. Instead, they are intended to help the reader achieve a deep-seated understanding bordering on epiphany: in Weber's terms, *verstehen.*

When Weber asked himself about salient distinctions between different systems of authority, he focused on what led people to ascribe authority to a given person. In some societies, the authority of rulers stems from the commitment of ordinary people to a regular, established, procedural system for selecting rulers and making collective decisions. Americans often say, "I voted for the other guy, but this is *our* president because *we* elected her." In effect, the person speaking is really saying "the system of rules matters, and the authority of the person in office has legitimacy grounded in our commitment to procedures." This is why the Florida election results of 2000 were so torturous for Americans of all political points of view. America has a political system based on what Weber called *rational–legal* authority grounded in the presumption most Americans have that the system of procedures is fair and will be followed. The people who were most bothered by the Florida election results were those, of whatever political party, who felt their own confidence in the electoral process being shaken or recognized the potential those events had for shaking the confidence of other people.

For a typology (meaning, a list of different types of something) to exist, there must be more than one common form. In addition to rational–legal authority, Weber identified two other common types of authority. One is *traditional authority,* in which the authority of rulers stems from a wide-spread commitment of ordinary people to the right of rule based on historical precedent. When someone says "God save the Queen" or "the ruling family knows what is best for us" or "the party will take care of us," they are, in essence, saying that the standing authority is legitimate because it is entrenched, and anyone who challenges entrenched authority is a subversive and not to be trusted or followed. Weber also noted a third type of authority, based on personal charisma. *Charismatic authority* rests on a cult of personality. That kind of legitimacy is grounded in personal magnetism.

Weber called attention to the fact that the type of authority prevailing at any given point in time has a big impact on what happens in society. And Weber correctly noted that cult of personality, such as that of Juan Peron in Argentina or Fidel Castro in Cuba, with the legitimacy of rule grounded in the magnetic appeal of a leader for some substantial number of citizens, can never be maintained for more than a few years or perhaps a few decades (only rarely, in fact, for more than a few years). Charismatic authority must eventually give way to some other basis of authority. Weber noted that a common trend in the twentieth century was for charismatic authority to temporarily replace traditional authority and to be replaced in turn by rational–legal authority.

Another example of Weber's ability to come up with analytical categories can be found in his work on *social rank.* Weber challenged the prevailing view among radicals of his time that economic position determines everything about a person's social station and political opportunities. Weber pointed out that social rank can be based on political position and social honor, as well as on economic resources. And he argued that these three bases of social ranking are largely independent of each other. Speaking of Germany at the time, Weber noted that a person's rank along one axis may be quite different from ranking along another axis. This was Weber's famous distinction between *class, status,* and *power.* To illustrate, he wrote convincingly that a poor person can be held in high esteem by virtue of having upstanding personal character, while a rich person can be despised as dishonest or uncaring. Of course, not all societies are the same, and in some places one's material well-being really does seem to dictate what judgments others will make of a person's worth. That is, after all, why conspicuous consumption can work as a status-seeking strategy in some societies, as Thorstein Veblen aptly noted.

Traditional, charismatic, and rational–legal authority, and class, status, and power as bases of social rank, are illustrations of Weber's use of the ideal-type method to categorize the different forms of phenomena such as status or authority. But Weber also used the method in another way. Ideal-types can be used to identify the most common characteristics of a particular organizational form. An example is *bureaucracy*. Using a modified ideal-type strategy, Weber looked at bureaucracy as one form of organization, and he identified the most common characteristics of that form. Approaching the topic in this way, Weber noticed that bureaucracies tend to be characterized by a basket of features: (a) hierarchical chain of command, (b) functional division of labor, (c) hiring based on training rather than nepotism, (d) decisions made according to a system of codified rules that are uniformly applied, and (e) records, as the property of offices rather than of office holders, being used to monitor performance and guide the development of new rules to further rationalize and improve operations. Bureaucracy was particularly important, from Weber's point of view, because it became the embodiment of rationalism as a value of modern (twentieth-century) industrial society. That is why bureaucracies tend to have a lot of rules. Rules are made to avoid repeating mistakes of the past, which is all very *rational*.

What seemed to Weber to be rational about bureaucracies was their ability to monitor performance and make rules designed to increase efficiency, maximize benefits, and most especially, minimize the repetition of costly errors. Of course, this assumes that feedback mechanisms are functioning properly, and that the organization has not been hijacked or subverted by special interests. Variations in the effectiveness of feedback mechanisms is an important sociological matter Weber never really addressed. He did, however, recognize that bureaucracies can become "iron cages" that trap people into sterile, inflexible responses that deaden individual creativity and can undermine individual involvement and personal responsibility. Bureaucracies can also discourage innovation, especially if people at the higher levels of the organization feel that subordinates may be launching activities that will be outside the control of superiors. These are all topics that continue to excite sociological discussion.

VALUES

Weber is most widely remembered for his analysis of the rise of capitalism in the West. He tried to explain why industrial capitalism really took hold in northwestern Europe rather than in China, which in several ways was a more likely place for it to have developed. After all, for centuries literacy was more widespread in China than in Europe, science was more advanced, commerce took place in what more closely approximated a single market, with villages linked by good river transportation, and political and administrative control were more centralized and more effective. But these advantages may have had a downside as well. Good communication and effective administration made it possible for the Chinese government to heavily tax profitable new businesses. Imperial tax policies seem to have sometimes stunted promising new enterprise rather than encouraging its development, especially when new enterprise was viewed with suspicion as a potential power base outside of the immediate control of the political establishment.

The most important difference between China and the West, in Weber's view, involved developments in Christianity fostering a "nondualistic economic ethic." Weber's argument was that what he interpreted to be Christianity's basic insistence that strangers should be treated the same way as neighbors, rather than victimized because of their vulnerability, helped facilitate the steady growth of long-distance trade that became the incubator of Western capitalism. Weber also believed that developments in Christianity fostered an asceticism encouraging frugality, which in turn encouraged saving, capital formation, and investment. Weber was originally convinced that Calvinism was responsible for this shift. He forcefully expressed this view in *The Protestant Ethic and the Spirit of Capitalism*, which was originally published as two separate works in 1904 and 1905.[3] Over the course of the next two decades, ending with *General Economic History*, published in 1923, Weber tempered his analysis a bit and came to believe that all of Christianity and in a way the whole of Judeo–Christian and arguably the Islamic tradition (not just Calvinism in any exclusive sense) was responsible for creating the preconditions for capitalism. Randall Collins explains this very nicely in a 1980 paper in the *American Sociological Review*.[4]

Weber's cultural determinism, with belief systems viewed as shaping economic events, is in stark contrast with Marx's economic determinism, which characterizes prevailing belief systems as reflections of the economic order and as instruments of ruling-class domination. In Weber's analysis, the values prevailing in a community are thought to exert a powerful and compelling force on people, shaping organizational forms and economic developments. This definitely differs from Marx, whose distinctive focus was economic power making it possible for rich people to manipulate public sentiment by hijacking government, mass media, ecclesiastic hierarchy, and other social institutions. Weber's insights on these matters can be expressed in the form of an axiom conveying his view that social structural arrangements embody, reflect, and reaffirm social values.

Values Axiom: *As a system of values becomes more deeply embedded and more uniformly held by people in a society, then institutional forms and relational patterns are progressively modified in ways that maximize adherence to core values.*

This axiom, which was integrated into later sociological analyses by Talcott Parsons (discussed in chapter 11), is accepted by some sociologists and contested by others. This is a good time to reiterate the fact that differences in metatheoretical perspectives are primarily defined by differences in the axiomatic assumptions different groups of theorists make. Developing a better theoretical understanding of the relationship between behavior and beliefs is one of the biggest challenges sociologists now face. And the Values Axiom, along with Weber's strategy of constructing idealtypes and recognizing the importance of historically unique particulars, left a lasting impact on subsequent generations of sociologists.

RECAP

There is general agreement that Max Weber is one of the most important sociologists to have ever lived. Weber successfully counteracted the Marxian premise that values are mere reflections of ruling-class strategy for controlling the masses. He catapulted values onto center stage as independent variables or intervening variables rather than as dependent variables in sociological models. Weber also influenced subsequent generations of sociologists by using the construction of ideal-types as a method for arriving at conceptual clarity that could lead to better understanding of sociological phenomena.

NOTES

1. Richard Mulcahy, *The Economics of Heinrich Pesch* (New York: Holt, 1952).
2. Max Weber, *From Max Weber*, edited by Hans Gerth and C. Wright Mills (New York: Oxford University Press, 1946).

3. Max Weber, *The Protestant Ethic and the Spirit of Capitalism* (1904–1905; reprint, New York: Scribner, 1930).
4. Randall Collins, "Weber's Last Theory of Capitalism: A Systemization," *American Sociological Review* 46, no. 6 (December 1980): 925–42.

SOME TERMS TO KNOW

Ideal-Type. A typological scheme used either (a) to categorize the major forms a certain kind of phenomenon can assume or (b) to identify the distinguishing characteristics of something.

Authority. The *legitimate* right to make certain kinds of decisions and expect those decisions to be carried out without resorting to threat of force.

Power. Ability to gain compliance through the threat or use of coercive force.

Rational. Characterized by forethought and calculated planning intended to minimize costs and negative side effects while maximizing benefits.

REVIEW OF AXIOM

Values Axiom: *As a system of values becomes more deeply embedded and more uniformly held by people in a society, then institutional forms and relational patterns are progressively modified in ways that maximize adherence to core values.*

CHAPTER REVIEW TEST

Check your answers in the back of the book. If you get any wrong, reread chapter 8, thinking about it as you go, before moving on to chapter 9.

1. An ideal-type
   a. identifies what the best and practically achievable forms are.
   b. identifies what the archetypical forms are.
   c. identifies what the impossible utopian forms are.

2. Weber's ideal-type of authority has three forms. What are they?

3. What are the characteristics of a bureaucratic organization as identified in Weber's ideal-type?

4. What is Weber's Values Axiom?

APPLICATION EXERCISE

Try developing an ideal-type by listing some common forms of nuclear families that are prevalent in the United States. Recognize that in order to do so, you must first narrow your conceptual ground. Are you, for example, more interested in defining who the members are (e.g., single-parent, cohabiting natural-parent, blended) or in defining the nature of role definitions (e.g., traditional, egalitarian)? Think about whether you have used the ideal-type method in a way that would help someone else think more clearly about differences that you feel are sociologically important, given the kinds of phenomena you want to understand. If so, the method has achieved its purpose.

9

AGENCY IN THE WORK OF GEORGE HERBERT MEAD

Individuals Working Together to Produce Social Reality

Far from the intellectual ferment of Western Europe, where lively discussion about macroeconomic change dominated the attention of pioneering sociologists, most of the first American sociologists were influenced by philosophy and psychology, and they were preoccupied with trying to understand how people adjust to each other in face-to-face human interaction. In the world's first sociology department, at the University of Chicago, their work coalesced in the viewpoints of George Herbert Mead. Mead's insights formed the bulwark of what would later come to be known as the "symbolic interactionist" perspective (discussed in chapter 13).

PRAGMATISM

The University of Chicago was founded with Rockefeller money at the end of the nineteenth century. Chicago was the rail hub of the nation. It viewed itself as a kind of spiritual as well as industrial heart of the United States during the era of industrialization. The Chicago World's Fair (the "World's Columbian Exposition") of 1892 and 1893 (precisely when the University of Chicago was forming the world's very first sociology department) marked a great celebration of optimism about things to come, symbolized by a huge dynamo, a generator for producing electrical current to make things happen.

The first administrators of the University of Chicago intentionally sought to hire faculty who would be intellectually bold and creative, and in this first-ever sociology department they certainly succeeded. A small group of sociologists centered at the University of Chicago produced theoretical breakthroughs of major importance in sociology: (a) formation of the symbolic interactionist perspective, treated in this chapter as well as in chapter 13, and (b) the development of urban ethnography as a methodological approach leading to significant theoretical developments, dealt with in chapter 10.

George Herbert Mead focused on a single, pivotal question: How do people manage to adjust to one another? This was a question of interest to psychologists and philosophers at the time, and Mead found himself in a circle of colleagues who were among the top minds of their era. One of those people was John Dewey, the person most often credited with America's most notable contribution to philosophy, *pragmatism*. Pragmatism stresses doing what works rather than sticking to failed models of the past. To illustrate in a way that has meaning for everyone, we can point out that Dewey was responsible for weakening the hold of the lecture style of teaching in schools by introducing field trips and emphasizing the importance of hands-on experience in K–12 education. Hands-on approaches work, Dewey argued, so we should use them. Do what works. That is pragmatism.

A pragmatic focus on what works was well suited to Chicago's dynamic character in the midst of America's industrialization. While New York may have been the nation's financial capital and Washington, D.C., its political center, Chicago was its rail hub and arguably its most diverse and robust manufacturing center. Pragmatism seemed to fit the city of Chicago's character at the time, but it also melded nicely with the ideas that were percolating in Mead's sociology at the University of Chicago.

THE SELF AS A PART OF SOCIAL SITUATION

To the pragmatist orientation borrowed from philosophy, the Chicago sociologists added a concern with "self-concept" drawn from the work of the most influential social psychologist of that era, William James. But the concept of "self" was given a less introspective psychological meaning and a decidedly more social flavor when employed by early sociologists such as Charles Horton Cooley at the University of Michigan. Remember the symbolic interactionist question is, How do people manage to adjust to one another? And recall the partial answer Mead drew from pragmatist philosophy: "Consider your situation, weigh the alternatives, select a path that may get you what you want, and get on that path." But what is the situation? And what does one really want? The psychologist William James recognized that the *self* each of us brings to a setting, with all of our personal drive and our baggage of personality, actually becomes a part of the setting.

Sociologist Charles Horton Cooley, in his 1902 book, *Human Nature and the Social Order*, provided what is for sociology an absolutely pivotal insight by recognizing the social origins, in other words the group origins, of self. Cooley's insight came when he realized that people think of themselves in ways that mirror how they believe themselves to be seen by others.[1] This was Cooley's famous concept of "looking-glass" (or mirror) self. Cooley recognized, for example, that children who daydream a lot and are then called "dumb" or "slow" or "retarded" by family members, teachers, schoolmates, or neighbors are at risk of growing up questioning their own abilities. Once that happens, those children may have difficulty ever gaining confidence in their own intellectual ability. Self-concept can be heavy baggage.

Sometimes, we are conscious of how we see ourselves; that is, we see ourselves as objects. At other times, how we really see ourselves is buried deep in the recesses of the subconscious. In either case, we all have certain awareness of ourselves, although our sense of self may or may not be entirely accurate. Awareness of ourselves definitely seems to flow in some manner out of the way in which others have responded to us in the past, and it influences our process of adjustment in day-to-day interaction with other people. Each of us carries our conception of self as a form of baggage, and each of us continually updates a portrait of our situational self, reflecting how we feel we are doing in the eyes of others. How we respond to situations is, to some extent, a function of what kinds of people we believe ourselves to be in general, and is also a function of how we feel we are performing in the immediate setting. For example, people who feel themselves to be clumsy are less likely to try new things when the opportunity unexpectedly arises. And people who crave more respect yet really do doubt their own ability tend to react according to these feelings. They may, for example, be particularly sensitive to anything that could be interpreted as a sign of being slighted. Thus, our sense of self in the situation can influence how we react.

Self-concept, then, deals with seeing oneself as an object. It is an individual's perception of her own fairly enduring qualities (such as degree of physical attractiveness, strength, speed, endurance, coordination, cleverness, memory, intellectual sharpness), in combination with the individual's assessment of her own immediate performance in the situation. Contemporary sociologists also focus on "identity," which is a sense of having a highly meaningful membership in a group, or a highly salient sense of belonging to a certain category of people. But "identity" does not have exactly the same meaning as "self-concept." "Self-concept" denotes qualities we feel we have that are essential to our own character as individuals or reflective of our own current performance potential as individuals. "Self" has to do with what makes us unique in comparison with people who are otherwise similar (other young African American men or other college-educated white women). "Identity" refers to a group or categorical membership (e.g., gender) that is highly salient and inescapably important, usually because others react to us in terms of that group membership rather than in terms of our truly individual qualities and character traits. Identity becomes salient to the degree that the groups that we are a part of seem to matter a lot to others. Identity captures how we have come to expect to be treated because of our appearance or our memberships, without regard to the true nature of our individual beliefs, actions, or performance.

Most sociologists take it as axiomatic that self and identity mirror our treatment from others.

Self/Identity Axiom: *The individual traits people think of themselves as having, and the memberships that people regard as salient, reflecting how people have responded to us in the past.*

This axiom relates well to Veblen's very important insight that all people want respect and are deeply conscious of their own social acceptance or lack of it. The hunt for acceptance is at the heart of the human social condition and human social experience.

Being part of a particular group or social category (e.g., gender, age, race/ethnicity, religion, gang membership, profession) can be tremendously important in how others treat us and in how we come to believe we will be treated. But understanding identity is complicated by our difficulty in disentangling identity from self. It is also complicated by the fact that people will frequently magnify an identity out of self-defense, after being stigmatized or excluded by others.

It is important to recognize that, on some level, sense of self, like one's sense of identity, is a kind of baggage we carry with us from place to place. If two people have trouble reaching for something and a person who happens to be watching begins to laugh, possible reactions vary, depending on the self-concept held by those persons who are unsuccessful with their reach in this situation. The laughter may be entirely unrelated to these two people straining to reach for something, but tell that to someone who is sensitive about matters of height. We all carry baggage, but seldom stop to calculate how that baggage may influence our perceptions and alter our behavior. When a person is accused of being "too sensitive" about something, it often means we are getting close to the heart of a portion of that person's self-concept or identity. People who are particularly sensitive about height are usually those who have been made, by others, to be acutely aware of their height. How we have come to view ourselves as objects does influence how we interpret and respond to situations. And those who are particularly sensitive about race are usually those who have been made aware, by others, that much of the world still reacts to what is on the outside (race or gender or age) instead of what is on the inside (character—honesty, empathy, responsibility, altruism, sincerity).

GEORGE HERBERT MEAD'S THEORETICAL SYNTHESIS

A handful of very bright people with a handful of very good ideas all came together at the same time and in the same intellectual community at the University of Chicago. Intellectual ferment was bubbling over in sociology at Chicago in the years around 1920. A synthesis was about to emerge, and George Herbert Mead was the person who would put this revealing new synthesis together. Mead synthesized a number of different ideas to describe the process that goes on as people adjust to each other during interpersonal communication.[2] Mead came to realize that people adapt cooperatively to the social world, and also actively remake their social worlds, by engaging in an ongoing five-step process during interaction:

1. People observe the gestures of others, taking note of verbal and nonverbal cues.

2. While observing some gestures, people decipher those gestures. This includes a process of orienting to "the role of the other" person to better understand what the other person actually wants and intends. Sociologists call this "role taking."

3. Role taking simultaneously invokes some degree of self-reflection. We have a core sense of self that we carry from situation to situation, and by triangulating on the reactions of other people toward us, we gain some degree of fluid "situational self-concept" about how our performance in the immediate situation might be viewed.

4. After "taking the role of the other" and also gaining some sense of the way we appear to others in the immediate situation, each of us is able to "imaginatively rehearse" different lines of potential conduct and select a path we judge has the best chance of producing the results we want, or at least ending in an outcome we find acceptable. This would include the face-saving work of departing a situation after presenting a sense of self that we feel is accurate and/or resembles the way we would like to be seen.

5. Having gone through these various mental exercises based on interpretation of the actions of others, we must then take the step of modifying our own contact as we continue the interaction.

Most sociologists accept the accuracy of this five-step description of the recurring process we go through as we adjust to others in daily life. It was as an unprecedented tribute to the power of Mead's ideas that his most important books, including *Mind, Self, and Society* (1934), were not actually written by Mead. They are collections of class notes that his students compiled and published under his name after his death. Mead's students collected their class notes and published them in book form under his name, because they recognized both the originality and the enormous importance of his contribution to sociology and to sociological theory.

Mead believed that one's ability to engage in symbolic interaction required a set of social skills that had to be learned. Human beings are not born knowing how to understand language or interpret most gestures. We are not born understanding how to identify roles or interpret what role another person is assuming. People must learn how to read gestures and to "role take," and we typically learn these crucial social skills during childhood play. For infants, interaction with caregivers is particularly important for learning the meaning of words and gestures. As children grow, interaction with peers becomes more important, especially when playing games (such as baseball) in which each person occupies a different role and has to be aware of the roles other players are simultaneously playing. Acquiring the social skills necessary to play these games empowers individuals with what Mead described as the capacity of "mind," which is the ability to adjust our actions in light of the responses of others. Ipso facto, we become true *social* beings capable of the constant adjustments social life requires.

A clear presumption built into Mead's analysis is that individuals have what sociologists sometimes term "agency," or free will, with the power to alter the flow of events. People make decisions about how to react to situations. Each individual has the power to alter relationships and change social meaning. Mead concentrated on the way people respond to immediate situations and how these responses subsequently change the flow of events and transform the understandings people have about events.

The daily relevance of Mead's ideas become apparent when we try to customize the way in which our role relationships with other people are defined. Right now, my own role as husband includes about 15 percent of the cooking and 65 percent of the kitchen cleaning. There have been times when I was expected to do more and times when I was not expected to do as much. Each long-term shift in role responsibilities involves a period of complex negotiated adjustment tied to other things, including child supervision, pet care, yard work, income-generating activity, elder care, community commitments, and personal maintenance, such as exercise. How does a particular definition of responsibility emerge? And when will people have the most or the least latitude in customizing their role obligations? Once a definition does emerge, how is it sustained? Mead gives us some answers that can be stated in the form of a principle.

Principle of Role Redefinition: *Other things being equal, people have the greatest latitude for customizing role relationships when (a) symbolic interaction is most frequent, longest lasting, and emotionally most intense; (b) people enjoy autonomy and perform their roles without much direct observation by others; (c) anticipatory socialization and validation for conventional performance are relatively weak; (d) peer group support of customization is clear; and (e) everyone involved in the relationship wants to redefine roles in the same direction.*

This principle gives us a way of understanding how much customization of roles will take place, although the Principle of Role Redefinition does not tell us what the outcomes of role redefinition will be. We will revisit this question in chapter 13.

APPRECIATING MEAD'S GENIUS

How do people manage to adjust to one another? Mead's answer is that people use their social skills to consider their situations, recognize their own roles in those situations, weigh the alternatives, select different paths, and try to negotiate with others to redefine commitments and expectations. If this idea seems rather ordinary and pedestrian, one has only to remember the ideas that had previously prevailed in order to appreciate the genius of Mead and his colleagues.

Social science before Mead was typified by the work of Italian criminologist Cesare Lombroso. Lombroso was a humanitarian who believed society should treat criminals with care and compassion because many criminals, he argued, were actually protohuman rather than fully human. He thought many people were in jail because they were not very far evolved beyond the apes and, as a result, were impulsive, lacking control over their basic animal instincts. In these cases, Lombroso did not see criminal behavior as a matter of free will exercised by callous people. His view was that the poor creatures just couldn't help themselves. The poor beasts should be isolated from society (to protect society) but treated with genuine compassion.

To put it politely, Lombroso's views sound extreme to a modern ear. But his ideas were consistent with the conventional wisdom of his time. In fact, he was viewed as being rather progressive. And remember that Lombroso (1836–1909) was only a few years older than Mead (1863–1931). Mead's ideas and those of his contemporaries marked a dramatic change in the accepted way of making sense of human behavior. If Lombroso's ideas seem silly and the ideas of Dewey and Mead and Cooley seem commonplace, it is because the insights of Mead and his colleagues were such an obvious improvement that they were fully absorbed by society. Their uncommonly perceptive insights have become our common sense. But that "common sense" was actually a striking departure from the world as most people understood it one hundred years ago, when the prevailing view was that behavior was for the most part dictated by genetic tendencies. Bad boys were thought to be bad because it was "in the blood."

RECAP

Early European sociology focused on what was outside the individual and in some sense predetermined by social forces beyond a person's control. Of course, European sociologists understood that Americans were right when they said people have "agency." Likewise, American sociologists understood that Europeans were right when they said many of the features of social reality we have to deal with were created without any help from us as specific individuals and would still be a part of the social landscape, even if a completely different set of people were here to contend with them. Micro and meso and macro dynamics are all important.

What Mead's work brought to sociology was an understanding of individual agency, which marked a dramatic advance. He brought an understanding that people really do have agency and a recognition of ways agency plays itself out in our daily interaction. An important element in this picture is how we see ourselves as a reflection of the way others have responded to us in the past. Once formed, self-concept and sense of identity are kinds of baggage we carry with us from situation to situation and that influence our interpretation of, and our reaction to, each new situation. In the mix of interpersonal communication that takes place, people are able to use their interaction skills to collect information about, reflect on, negotiate in regard to, and adjust their conduct with others. In fact, we are constantly doing these things, which is why many sociologists are convinced that George Herbert Mead's work tells us about the very heart of what it means to be a social being engaged in social life.

NOTES

1. Charles Horton Cooley, *Human Nature and the Social Order* (New York: Scribner, 1902).
2. George Herbert Mead, *Mind, Self, and Society* (Chicago: University of Chicago Press, 1934).

SOME TERMS TO KNOW

Self-Concept. A sense of one's own being as a distinctly separate person having particular internal qualities and tending to perform in certain ways.

Identity. A sense of having a highly meaningful membership in a group or highly salient association with a category of people.

Role Taking or *"Taking the Role of the Other."* Recognizing what role another person is in, what objectives they have, and what constraints they face.

Agency. Free will, with the power to alter the flow of events.

REVIEW OF AXIOM AND PRINCIPLE

Self/Identity Axiom: *The individual traits people think of themselves as having, and the memberships that people regard as salient, reflecting how people have responded to us in the past.*

Principle of Role Redefinition: *Other things being equal, people have the greatest latitude for customizing role relationships when (a) symbolic interaction is most frequent, longest lasting, and emotionally most intense; (b) people enjoy autonomy and perform their roles without much direct observation by others; (c) anticipatory socialization and validation for conventional performance are relatively weak; (d) peer group support of customization is clear; and (e) everyone involved in the relationship wants to redefine roles in the same direction.*

CHAPTER REVIEW TEST

Check your answers in the back of the book. If you get any wrong, reread chapter 9, thinking about it as you go, before moving on to chapter 10.

1. What was Mead's central question?

2. Match theorists with the concepts they have come to be identified with:
   a. Charles Horton Cooley   1) pragmatism
   b. John Dewey   2) looking-glass self

3. Differentiate between self-concept and identity.

4. Describe the process of symbolic interaction people work through as they adjust to others.

APPLICATION EXERCISE

Describe a role relationship you are familiar with that has been redefined over time. What can you say about the process of role redefinition as it unfolded in that particular relationship? Based on what you have observed, can you suggest any improvements in the Principle of Role Redefinition? Did the events you observed suggest anything about the self-concept or salient identities of anyone involved? Do you believe either self-concept or identity had any impact on the way in which roles were redefined over time?

10

CHICAGO COMMUNITY STUDIES AND THE BIRTH OF URBAN ETHNOGRAPHY

As George Herbert Mead was beginning his work, several of his colleagues and many of their graduate students at the University of Chicago were pioneering the development of urban ethnography as a research method. Urban ethnography is the research technique of carefully observing how people go about their daily lives within a community, in order to describe community life thoroughly while developing an analysis of how people are interconnected, how decisions are made, and how basic needs are met. Urban ethnography is a sociological innovation.

THE BEGINNING OF URBAN ETHNOGRAPHY

Ethnographic techniques were first used at about the same time by early sociologists and anthropologists. However, anthropologists initially restricted the use of ethnographic techniques to small hunting and gathering bands and concentrated their attention on food gathering and spiritual/religious observances. Use of ethnographic techniques to study larger communities, especially urban neighborhoods, and to investigate the more complex and varied range of community-based phenomena that urban neighborhoods produce, began in sociology around 1900. By way of contrast, it was not until the 1970s that urban ethnography assumed a relatively high profile in sociology's sister discipline of anthropology.

The pioneers of urban ethnography were Robert Park and his colleagues in sociology at the University of Chicago, W. E. B. DuBois and his colleagues in sociology at Atlanta University, and Robert and Helen Merrell Lynd working in Muncie, Indiana (discussed in chapter 12). Urban ethnography came to be emblematic of sociological research. And more of this work was done in Chicago than in any other city. As the nineteenth century drew to a close, Chicago was a magnet for people from all around the world. This made it the perfect field laboratory for sociological investigation.

Sociology's urban ethnographers were intrigued by the fact that cities were constantly being recreated by successive waves of arrivals from the countryside or from other countries. What emerged was a clear pattern of neighborhood succession as one group of people replaced another. Chicago sociologists observing this as an ongoing process chronicled a regular cycle of community disorganization and reorganization over time.

Comprehensive studies of ethnic neighborhoods began just after 1900. Some of the best illustrations of this work are Thomas and Znaniecki's two-volume 1918 work, *The Polish Peasant in Europe and America*, and Louis Wirth's 1928 study of the divide between German and Eastern European Jewish neighborhoods, *The Ghetto*.[1] Sociology's growing ranks of urban ethnographies detailed the structure of communities and the lives of people in them. A recurrent theme in sociology's urban ethnographies was that when large numbers of people find themselves uprooted and moving to a new land, they reshape and reformulate their identities as they try to reconstruct some semblance of the communities and cultures they left behind. This reconstruction always takes the form of a creatively adaptive hybrid, retaining things that are useful for helping people face the barriers and difficulties they confront in their new environment and abandoning some practices that serve no purpose for life in the new setting.

A key insight of sociology's urban ethnographies is that adaptation of old forms is often quite functional. One illustration can be found in social groups drawing together migrants from a single region to enjoy music and update old friends on life events. These groups often take on functions as employment agencies and savings and loan organizations. In ethnic communities, we also see special stress placed on things that comfort people or help in affirming identity. Bakeries, for example, can have more importance to people struggling with identity in a hostile environment than they do in places of origin, where one's identity is taken for granted and secure.[2]

Sociology's urban ethnographers have always been intrigued by the fact that people, even those without many resources, adapt old beliefs and practices to fit new conditions and affirm their own dignity and distinctive identity, even as their ways of thinking and acting begin to diverge greatly from those of their ancestors.[3] This pivotal insight can be captured in the form of an axiom.

Cultural Adaptation Axiom: *Migrants change a great deal during migration, and they are highly selective in the aspects of culture they retain and highly innovative in how they modify those aspects of culture to meet new needs.*

Here we see another clear expression of pragmatism in the intellectual outlook dominating Chicago sociology. The community patterns that Chicago sociologists noticed being institutionalized in immigrant neighborhoods were those that filled a need. Immigrants who claim to be traditionalists are sometimes the most active change agents, altering old patterns of association for new purposes and helping people deal with an inhospitable social climate where they find themselves to be aspiration heavy and resource poor.

THE PAIN OF THE COUNTRY, THE LURE OF THE CITY

Sociology's early urban ethnographies almost always seemed to focus on the efforts of migrating groups to form communities. Sometimes, those groups were immigrants coming from a particular country, as in the case of Thomas and Znaniecki's *The Polish Peasant in Europe and America*. Sometimes they were internal migrants siphoned from one geographic area into another. This was the case in W. E. B. DuBois's study *The Philadelphia Negro*.[4] DuBois is an important figure in American history. He was the first African American to receive a Ph.D. in any field from any American university (sociology—Harvard University). He went on to conduct pioneering research (not in Chicago, but in Philadelphia and Atlanta) exposing many aspects of the American condition that had been overlooked or ignored. He was a major contributor to the development of urban ethnographic techniques in sociology, and in the process he made important contributions to the Civil Rights Movement in the years leading up to the rise of Martin Luther King.

Some of the urban ethnographers focused on migrants of a particular demographic group, usually unattached young males. This was the case with Nels "Bo" Anderson's study *The Hobo*.[5] These rootless young men were of special interest to readers, and Anderson's study of them helped bring legitimacy and acclaim to early sociology. In 1900, few people went to college, and many young men (and some young women) from poor families "hit the road" with nothing in their pockets but hope. At that time, there were waves of economic refugees from the declining farm economy. Places such as Chicago were magnets, attracting young men who had no promise of advancement where they were and came to the city in search of jobs and excitement.

The urban ethnographies of migrants in Chicago gave rise to a new understanding about the causes of migration. Despite outward appearances, interviews made it clear that few people leave their homes only because of poverty or persecution. There must also be some enticement, the "pull" of opportunities for better jobs, more excitement, better public services, easier access to health care, or higher culture. Conversely, few people leave their homes only because of "pull" factors, that is, those making a distant destination enticing. Most people must also be "pushed" by economic hardship or persecution of some sort. Thus, the famous "push/pull" theory of migration (migration increases as a positive function of (a) the pull of opportunities or excitement, added to (b) the push of poverty or persecution), which is really just a concrete expression of the Rational Action Principle. People generally make calculations based on a range of comparative costs and benefits, rather than acting in response to a single precipitating event.

SOCIAL PROBLEMS AND SOCIOLOGICAL THEORY

There is often a seedy side to sociology's urban ethnographies. The influx of rootless young men changes neighborhoods in ways a lot of people do not like. Substance abuse, prostitution, fighting, gambling, and burglary are all more common in the grimy rooming-house neighborhoods where rootless people typically congregate. University of Chicago sociologists were right there to report on the ways those neighborhoods were being transformed. And much of the transformation being chronicled had to do with (positive) reorganization rather than (negative) disorganization. Anderson's work described the day-labor system of the skid row community, close to the downtown, and the barber colleges along Halsted Street, which held out hope in the guise of entry-level employment training. And for single young men with no money and no prospects there were safe dance halls where an uprooted young man could enjoy fleeting moments of contact with women for a dime a dance.[6] Substance abuse was a widespread problem. But the urban ethnographies that sociologists wrote tended to offer an understanding of drug culture rooted in an appreciation of the basic humanity of substance abusers.[7] Research of this kind led to the development of intervention and rehabilitation programs that had some success in dealing with otherwise intractable issues. Sociology makes a constructive difference. Social support is the single most important part of any successful battle against substance abuse.

Chicago sociology was interwoven with social work at that time. Jane Addams, founder and operator of Hull House and later winner of a Nobel Prize, was associated with the sociology program at the University of Chicago. Even at that early stage, sociology programs were practicing community-based learning and advocating purposeful education to empower students to help build a better society and not just engage in intellectual navel gazing.

NEIGHBORHOOD TRANSITION

An accompanying discovery made by sociology's urban ethnographies is that neighborhoods change very rapidly at one point in the neighborhood succession process. As in-migration accelerates, marginal neighborhoods can fill up and spill over with poor people, fueling intergroup antagonism and conflict. More-affluent, better-established people move into nicer neighborhoods, opening the path for a wider invasion by people at the bottom rungs of the socioeconomic ladder. Spillover of members of one community onto the territory of another usually starts slowly. But when a "tipping point" of about 30 percent is reached, locals see that the old neighborhood is going to change whether they like it or not, and they begin to abandon it in droves. The "white flight" phenomenon illustrates this pattern. By the time the neighborhood is 85 percent changed, the rate of change slows because everyone who is eager to leave and has the means to leave has already gone. Neighborhood gentrification trends, in which young, upwardly mobile people lay claim to a dilapidated old neighborhood, can also bump along at fits and starts until a tipping point is reached, after which time it is almost impossible for old-time residents to find affordable housing. If you have almost no income and you live in

San Francisco or Vancouver, it is getting harder and harder to find place to live, because more and more of the buildings poor people once lived in are being taken over and renovated for those who have the ability to pay high rents.

The Chicago sociologists also discovered that community dynamics are constrained by the commercial geography of the city. When Robert Park, Ernest Burgess, and Roderick McKensie wrote *The City* in 1925, the pattern of ethnic succession was clear and a concentric-zone model of the urban ecology of Chicago had become apparent. Business services were concentrated in the downtown center. Factories were clustered close enough to downtown to benefit from transit hubs, but far enough away to minimize rents. Transients and organized criminal activity were heavily concentrated in a densely populated but geographically thin sandwich of land between downtown and the factories. Ethnic neighborhoods of factory workers were interspersed with or located just beyond the factories. And somewhat more prosperous people lived farther away to escape the grimy coal dust that coated everything in Chicago prior to widespread conversion to cleaner-burning natural gas around 1960.[8]

Government has the potential for changing urban ecology by influencing where and how needs are met and tastes are satisfied. But oftentimes the impacts of government intervention are unforeseen. When the city of Chicago closed down its geographically localized and centrally placed red-light district where vice was concentrated, political leaders were surprised by the results. (If they had asked a sociologist what would happen, they might not have been so surprised.) Sex commerce moved into smaller and less-obvious locations sprinkled all around the city and into neighboring communities. Similarly, when alcohol was made illegal during prohibition, Al Capone and other bootleggers opened a string of speakeasies that everyone knew about and that were very popular as public entertainment centers for adults from all social strata.

Sociologists on the street identified new trends and saw unintended consequences right from the start. This is a big reason why sociologists sometimes seem to be out of the mainstream, politically speaking. Part of our job is to recognize trends as they are beginning and to sound an early warning of more serious consequences to come. This is unpopular with those who would rather shoot the messenger than address the problem. But part of our job really is to do what we can to try to make sure festering realities are understood before problems mushroom out of control. As a practical matter, this means that sociological research frequently gives voice to the voiceless.

RECAP

In the early twentieth century, when what it meant to be a sociologist and do sociology was being defined, sociology's urban ethnographies were leaving a lasting legacy. Their focus was on naturalistic observation of real people in their community settings, on taking the pulse of the community, and on celebrating the way ordinary people live. In the process, we learned that communities are constantly changing. Even if a community suffers through a period of decline, people there are always inventing new community arrangements. We also learned that vice is like a squishy water balloon. If pressure is applied to constrict vice in one neighborhood, the vice tends to migrate elsewhere instead of disappearing. It may become less visible for a time, or it may change its form. But it typically does not simply evaporate.

NOTES

1. William I. Thomas and Florian Znaniecki, *The Polish Peasant in Europe and America* (Urbana: University of Illinois Press, 1918); Louis Wirth, *The Ghetto* (Chicago: University of Chicago Press, 1928).

2. Ivan Light, *Ethnic Enterprise in America* (Berkeley: University of California Press, 1972).

3. Robert Park and Herbert Miller, *Old World Traits Transplanted* (New York: Harper & Row, 1921). W. I. Thomas authored major portions of this work, but he is not mentioned as a coauthor. At the time the book was being readied for publication, Thomas had some bad press relating to events in his personal life. Thomas did not want his association with the book to slow its release. People in the sociological community understood this at the time.

4. W. E. B. DuBois, *The Philadelphia Negro* (1899; reprint, New York: Schocken, 1967).

5. Nels Anderson, *The Hobo: The Sociology of the Homeless Man* (Chicago: University of Chicago Press, 1923).

6. Paul Cressey, *The Taxi-Dance Hall* (Chicago: University of Chicago Press, 1932).

7. Alfred Lindesmith, *Addiction and Opiates* (Chicago: Aldine, 1968).

8. Robert Park, Ernest Burgess, and Roderick McKenzie, *The City* (Chicago: University of Chicago Press, 1925).

REVIEW OF AXIOM

Cultural Adaptation Axiom: *Migrants change a great deal during migration, and they are highly selective in the aspects of culture they retain and highly innovative in how they modify those aspects of culture to meet new needs.*

CHAPTER REVIEW TEST

Check your answers against the answer key at the end of the book. If you get any wrong, reread chapter 10, thinking about it as you go, before moving on to chapter 11.

1. Match authors with their topics.

   a. Nels Anderson

   b. Al Lindesmith

   c. W. I. Thomas and Florian Znaniecki

   d. Louis Wirth

   1. Jewish immigrant neighborhoods
   2. Polish Catholic immigrant neighborhoods
   3. Lives of homeless men
   4. Drug addiction

2. When does the tipping point seem to be reached in neighborhood succession?

3. What does the Cultural Adaptation Axiom tell us?

APPLICATION EXERCISE

Take a bus ride or a walk through a neighborhood you do not often venture into. This should be a neighborhood with enough street activity that you can see something. Observe some things that seem different from what you are accustomed to. Ask yourself what you think these things mean. This, of course, is just a taste of urban ethnography. Urban ethnographers spend time to make sure they are known and accepted and have sources of support in the community they plan to conduct research in. Then they might spend years immersed in the community, talking to people, actively engaging in participant observation, really becoming a part of the scene.

Part III

Making Sense of Sociology's Theoretical Paradigms: Grasping the Basics

In part I of this book, we explored the meaning of theory in a science. Theory is activity aimed at clearly expressing how we think differences are produced. The differences sociologists are interested in are differences in the nature of (a) interpersonal attachments, (b) shared beliefs, and (c) systemic interconnections, including regulatory constraints. When we practice sociology *as a science*, we try to describe those three things (attachments, shared beliefs, and systemic interconnections and constraints); to understand the dynamic processes that give rise to differences within or between settings over time; to understand how and why consequences result from having particular kinds of interpersonal attachments, shared beliefs, or systemic interconnections and constraints; and finally, to utilize our growing body of knowledge for helping groups and organizations operate more effectively and for the purpose of promoting community-level institution building for the common good.

We know we are making progress in identifying theory when we can express axioms and principles that, after research and refinement, enhance our ability to explain social reality. Research is activity designed to test axioms and principles using real-world data, with the conviction that testing our ideas will allow us to refine and improve our understanding. That is the scientific process.

In part II of this book we discussed seminal works of the key intellectual pioneers who launched sociology as a discipline. With historical hindsight, we can see that the most important of these figures were Emile Durkheim, George Herbert Mead, and Max Weber, who all self-consciously recognized themselves as sociologists (although Weber began his academic career as an economist, Mead was heavily influenced by philosophy and psychology, and Durkheim held a joint appointment in education), and Karl Marx, who always thought of himself as an economist or political economist, but nevertheless contributed in very important ways to the base of theoretical insights that have motivated subsequent sociological investigation. Most sociological research unfolds in the tradition established by these four pivotal figures, along with insights drawn from the utilitarian economists and developed by sociology's urban ethnographers.

Durkheim, Marx, Weber, and Mead were most important as first founders because they asked the big questions that have captured sociologists' attention over the years: (a) In what ways does society impose itself on the individual, and how do we understand that process (Durkheim)? (b) How is it that segments of the society become polarized against each other, and with what long-term consequences does this happen (Marx)? (c) To what extent do values dictate how people will construct their social world, and to what extent do values reflect and mirror a construction of the social world that is already in place (Weber)? (d) How do individual people adjust to others and exert agency over the course of events (Mead)?

People thinking about sociology's big questions have carried the work of the first founders forward in a variety of directions, coalescing into four distinct and recognizable perspectives. The first of these developed around the time of World War II, when the insights of European sociologists and economists were being synthesized by Talcott Parsons and others into a structural–functionalist framework influenced most by Durkheim, Weber, Pareto, and the British utilitarian economists. By the late 1950s, partly in response to what were seen as the blind spots of American structural–functionalism, conflict theory and symbolic interactionism coalesced out of work being done to extend the basic insights of Marx, Weber, and Mead. Somewhat later, exchange theory emerged out of an amalgamation of concerns raised by the people working in each of the other emerging traditions.

Part III attempts to offer very brief and manageable introductions to these four perspectives. Our goal is to provide a useful framework for firmly grasping the basics. As in the earlier sections of the book, part III is intentionally brief. It is skeletal by design, in order to retain clear and explicit focus on the most fundamental points. We promote conceptual clarity by staying away from the sort of all-encompassing detail that can make it hard for people to arrive at a holistic understanding.

11

TALCOTT PARSONS AND STRUCTURAL–FUNCTIONALISM MADE EASY

Systems Change When Needs Are Not Met

Each of the four theoretical perspectives covered in this part was formed as a creative synthesis of the ideas of several different theorists. Each is highly useful and illuminating once its central premises are properly understood. The chapters that follow convey main points in a clear way and do not attempt to cover much detail.

The first of sociology's paradigms to take definitive shape was structural–functionalism. By about 1955, the structural–functionalist perspective had assumed its basic form, but the creative inspiration for contemporary structural–functionalism can be traced to Harvard University in the 1930s, where it evolved out of intellectual activity swirling around Talcott Parsons. Parsons creatively integrated ideas he drew from Vilfredo Pareto, Emile Durkheim, and Max Weber, along with British utilitarian economists. This synthesis was one of the most intellectually ambitious efforts ever undertaken by a sociological theorist. Although Parsons's effort was not a total success, it is intriguing and marks an important point in sociology's disciplinary history.

Each of sociology's established theoretical paradigms offers revealing explanations of important sources of variation in the real world. Each of these paradigms has a metatheoretical core that consists of a set of sensitizing concepts and axiomatic assumptions that lead people to raise particular kinds of questions when employing their respective frameworks.

Structural–functionalists treat societies as social systems. They recognize that systems change in significant ways over time and believe societal change tends to be driven by a search for better ways of organizing activity to meet needs.

The most prominent "sensitizing concepts," the concepts structural–functionalists use to help them focus on the things they are interested in, are social system, social structure, institutionalization, culture, values, roles, norms, authority, legitimacy, fiduciary responsibility, feedback, equilibrium, regulation/deregulation, centralization/decentralization, functional need, and integration. Add these to the axiomatic assumptions structural–functionalists make and the questions they ask and we have structural–functionalism's metatheoretical framework. This framework grew out of sociologists' efforts to recognize and understand systemic tendencies for progressive change.

If you accept Comte's vision for the goal of sociology, which is acquisition of knowledge we can use to make society better, then understanding systemic tendencies for progressive change is critical. And importantly, understanding how progressive change comes about necessarily involves understanding how progressive change is quite frequently resisted and subverted. The fact is that you will have a hard time finding many structural–functionalists who think things get better over time because the world is made up entirely of warm-hearted humanists who want to do good things for their less fortunate neighbors. Nor will it be easy to find structural–functionalists who automatically assume people in power are benevolent, truth-seeking civil servants. It seems pretty clear to a structural–functionalist that, for every dozen of those, a number of vicious, self-serving liars find their way into the corridors of power. But if societies really are systems made up of interrelated domains, feedback mechanisms will be at work. Problematic decisions will have mounting consequences that will eventually be absorbed as costs for someone. That produces sources of "push back" that, in theory, make societies self-correcting systems. The goal of structural–functionalism must ultimately be to discover how those feedback and equilibrium processes operate on a societal level.

To that end, structural–functionalists have made some significant progress in developing explanatory principles, specifically those dealing with social control (chapter 4), hierarchy (chapter 5), and structural strain (this chapter). The main purpose of this chapter, however, is to reveal how structural–functionalists have come to view the world, and to gain an understanding about how the framework has evolved over time. In the process, we will also gain a clearer understanding of the work that remains to be done by people operating within that theoretical framework.

INTEREST IN VILFREDO PARETO AND HIS SYSTEM DEFINING EQUILIBRIA: THE "HARVARD PARETO CIRCLE"

To understand the development of structural–functionalism in the United States after 1930 requires that we remember the earlier theoretical contributions of Vilfredo Pareto, Max Weber, and Emile Durkheim. Vilfredo Pareto (France/Italy/Switzerland, 1848–1923) was a very famous economist (the "father of mathematical economics") known for his use of equilibrium modeling to understand changes in price and long-term trends in supply and demand. Between about 1887 and 1897, Pareto was consumed with the task of building mathematical models for economics. But with each passing year after 1897, he devoted more time to the study of sociological factors influencing the economy. He spent the last twenty years of his life trying to develop a sociological theory that lived up to Comte's "queen science" vision of the discipline: an overarching sociological theory that could subsume the study of economics and political science, more or less as subdisciplines within a grander and more encompassing sociological framework. Pareto did this by applying equilibrium analysis to the study of society as a holistic system composed of interdependent spheres of social, economic, and political activity, where each sphere is understood to have specific kinds of impacts on every other sphere. For example, Pareto thought economic prosperity changed social values so that people became more hedonistic and interested in short-term gratification. Then people saved less, interest rates went up, economic investment contracted, and people became more cautious and began to save again. Notice a "stable" equilibrium process, with change in one direction stimulating a series of reactions that eventually return the society to something approximating its prior state. At other times, we see "moving" equilibria at work, with change in one direction stimulating a series of reactions that moves things away from old equilibrium points to new ones. In Pareto's time, advances in steam engine technology for powering factories and railroads drove a moving equilibrium that produced dramatic change in a short period of time.

This was pretty exciting stuff for Pareto and many other sociologists of his era. They wanted to understand the economy (as well as trends in government reorganization and changes in social beliefs and practices) and felt that use of broad models involving socioeconomic mutual causality was the only way to do it. This was a bold intellectual move.

For Pareto, this was a tremendously exciting intellectual endeavor. He viewed society as a social system, with interdependent social, economic, and political domains. And he understood that by identifying ways in which social, economic, and political phenomena influenced each other, he could model societal change.

Pareto's concept of equilibrium involves the property of elasticity, or ability to increase or decrease quickly and easily in response to changing conditions. Sometimes there is only a little elasticity in a system and sometimes there is a great deal. For example, the United States has a large army, so the military enjoys a lot of flexibility in how it will deploy troops during relatively tranquil periods. But if hostilities cause large numbers of troops to be committed to battle or occupation, then at that point in time the military has less flexibility. Elasticity varies over time. When changing conditions require adjustment, some adjustment can be made with relative ease. Your army has a lot of extra troops; your country can send a few to country X without a strain. But if changing conditions continue to require more supplemental effort, elasticity can disappear and more dramatic steps are forced. You already have a lot of troops deployed in the occupation of Iraq and suddenly need more someplace else. There is no problem as long as you are willing to choose among reducing global military presence, instituting a draft, and finding more allies. Applying concepts such as elasticity and capacity constraint or feedback and equilibrium enable us to make sense of a lot of things that are important for us to understand.

Pareto's switch from economics to sociology came about because he wanted to include relevant sociological factors in his models. He was a real social scientist. Pareto's genius was in adopting equilibrium models for the study of the whole social system and not just the economy. He did so by examining the ways in which cyclical shifts between periods of regulation and deregulation in government, and cyclical shifts between periods of liberalism and conservatism in popular mood, influenced and were influenced by shifts in the business cycle.[1]

Pareto concluded that there is enough evidence of mutual impact among social, economic, and political spheres to justify conceptualizing society as a system. Pareto's equilibrium analysis of society as a system intrigued Joseph Henderson, who early in the twentieth century was a very influential senior professor of physiology at Harvard University. In the early 1930s, Henderson gathered a circle of bright young social scientists around him. These included George Homans, who would later become a major advocate of exchange theory in American sociology; Robert K. Merton, who arrived at Harvard familiar with the works of Durkheim before Durkheim's books had been translated from French into English; and Talcott Parsons, who arrived at Harvard familiar with the works of Max Weber before Weber's books had been translated from German into English. (In fact, Parsons was the first of Weber's translators for an English audience.) There were several other young social scientists in this circle. This discussion group, described in a 1968 paper by Barbara Heyl, was the seedbed that produced structural–functional thinking in American sociology.[2]

TALCOTT PARSONS BRINGS WEBERIAN CONTENT TO THE HARVARD PARETO CIRCLE

Talcott Parsons (United States, 1902–1979; Ph.D., University of Heidelberg, 1929) was studying in Germany shortly after the death of Max Weber and while Max Weber's brother, Alfred Weber, was still teaching sociology at a German university. Parsons became Weber's first major conduit into American sociology. Importantly, Parsons completely absorbed Weber's notion that the value system of a society has immense impact on events. This is captured in our Values Axiom (from chapter 8). And he fully adopted Weber's method of constructing ideal-types as a strategy for trying to better define analytical distinctions (also described in chapter 8).

Although a great synthesizer, Parsons was first and foremost a Weberian. Weber's analytical approach became deeply ingrained for Parsons when he studied in Germany. By the time he was recruited into the Harvard Pareto circle, Parsons was already a convincing advocate for Weber's position that societal values are among the most important things sociologists should be looking at.

Weber's work was Parsons's intellectual starting point; it was his foundation. You might say that Parsons added Durkheim's and Pareto's insights to that Weberian foundation. But there is another way to look at what was going on in Parsons's mind. Having the ideas of Durkheim and

Pareto swirling within the Harvard Pareto circle helped Parsons see how to bring more intellectual order to Weber's approach. In Parsons's view, Weber's work was too haphazard and in need of analytical focus and direction. Parsons found this in the main points Pareto and Durkheim emphasized. Society can be viewed as a social system (Pareto) in which needs have to be met (Durkheim). Structural forms evolve over time to meet those needs (Durkheim), and the nature of society as a system of interrelated domains means that the repercussions of any change can be tracked and then better understood (Pareto). These were all convictions Weber shared. But they remained implicit in his work. He never worked out their theoretical implications. Parsons saw working out these implications as his special task. Weber's concern with social values is at the heart of Parsons's scheme, but Parsons infuses his Weberian analysis with the awareness of society as a system that Durkheim made explicit.

PATTERN VARIABLES

Parsons, like Weber, wanted to treat values as variables. Doing so would mean finding a way of measuring quantitative or qualitative differences between systems of values prevailing in different places, or between the systems of values prevailing in one place at different points in time. Parsons was enough of a scientist to know that variables imply measurement, and that the act of measurement is a step on the road to conceptual clarity.

Parsons looked to Weber's work for guidance about measurement and found clues in Weber's discussion of qualitative differences in role expectations. Values have impact on what roles come to mean to role occupants and how those people live out their commitments in everyday life. So Parsons quite naturally looked to differences in roles as a source of information about qualitative differences in societal value systems. Since Parsons was trained in Weberian method, the next logical step he needed to take was to develop a categorical system he could use in his effort to identify qualitative differences in roles that might reflect deep cultural differences at work.

Parsons did this comparatively early in his career. The task occupies an important part of his 1951 book, *The Social System* (a title drawn from Pareto). In *The Social System*, Parsons offers what he calls a "pattern variables" scheme for contrasting the value systems of different societies.[3]

Parsons observed that the value system of every society could be placed on a series of continua. Following Weber, he observed that the way in which roles took shape in any one society reflected the core values of that society.

Parsons spoke of five different sets of pattern variables. For purposes of illustration, one is the continuum running between (a) "affectivity," or the degree to which people think it is good if role relations are characterized by a lot of strong emotional feeling and expression, and (b) "affective neutrality," or the degree to which people think it is good if role relations are characterized by some emotional distance and control. Germany and Italy do not fall at exactly the same point on this continuum, and we can see this by contrasting the same role in the two societies. What it means to be a teacher in Germany is slightly different from what it means in Italy, and this difference is in part a reflection of cultural standards about the qualities that are regarded as good and appropriate. Approached in this way, comparing roles could allow sociologists to identify qualitative differences in value systems separating different societies. Just how much emotional involvement are teachers supposed to have with their students? Not too much and not too little. But how much is deemed to be too much? And how little is deemed to be too little? That varies from society to society. Parsons felt those questions were answered in each society by its particular constellation of values. The amount considered just about right in one country may not be seen as appropriate in another country. And Parsons understood that we really knew something about societal values if, in contrasting the same kinds of roles in two different societies, we started to see recurring patterns reflecting the fact that many roles involved more expression of emotion in Italy than those same roles in Germany, and many roles involved more control of emotion in Germany than those same roles in Italy.

Following Weber, and also Mead, Parsons was keenly interested in ways that the rights and obligations that are built into roles both reflect and reaffirm particular societal values. Parsons used a total of five sets of pattern variables. These were (1) affectivity, or preference for feeling and expressing emotional bond in role encounters, versus affective neutrality, or preference for minimizing the expression and even the experience of emotional bond in role encounters; (2) universalism, or preference for uniform standards applied to everyone in the same way, versus particularism, or preference for having differences in standards as appropriate for different groups; (3) specificity, or preference for imposing limited and well-defined obligations on a role, versus diffuseness, or preference for expecting role occupants to respond to a wide array of demands that are not always clearly defined; (4) ascription, or preference for allocating opportunities and assignments on the basis of demographic memberships (e.g., gender, ethnicity) and family or origin (e.g., class), versus achievement, or allocating opportunities and assignments on the basis of individual performance; and (5) a fifth set of pattern variables that appears early in Parsons's work but was dropped for analytical reasons in his latter work, that is, self, or society's value preference that individuals be oriented toward pursuit of individual goals and benefits, versus collectivity, or society's value preference that individuals be oriented toward the achievement of collective ends.

DURKHEIM'S WORK SUGGESTS A
STRUCTURAL–FUNCTIONAL FRAMEWORK

Parsons thought of values and roles as major components of the "structure" we organize our lives around. Using the Weberian orientation that he had when he arrived on Harvard's faculty fresh from graduate school in Germany, Parsons then added Durkheim's concept of "function" by asking what consequences each structural difference has. What consequences does a particular configuration of values have for the society as a whole? Parsons and other structural–functionalists tended to assume that particular constellations of values emerge for a reason, and it is important to articulate this as an assumption.

Form Follows Function Axiom: *Form follows function in the sense that widespread patterns of structural change emerge as systemic responses to meet new needs or correct for poor performance in the face of old needs.*

This general mode of thinking is standard to the structural–functionalist intellectual framework. Remember that axioms are analytical devices that help us look for things that may be important. They are not taken to be *absolute* truths, even by the theorists who use them. Not everything is functional. But thinking about what would happen if the natural flow of events were toward functionality helps us identify both convergent and divergent cases, which we can then study for important clues about the way the world does work. This is science. Try to describe how things work in theory. Then we can collect the data necessary to test old explanations and move on to better, more penetrating, more revealing descriptions of how the world works and explanations of why it works that way.

It makes sense to look for dysfunctions. Robert K. Merton was particularly skilled at looking for negative side effects. He offered a scheme for conducting structural–functional analysis that was more open than the one Parsons developed. Merton advocated that sociologists examine every aspect of structure asking two very generic functional questions: (1) What are the negative as well as the positive consequences? (2) To what degree are consequences planned and intended, and to what degree are they unplanned and unintended?[4] Asking these questions, Merton discovered that there are a lot of unintended negative consequences in the world. Those negative unintended consequences are of real interest to sociologists, both as data to help us better understand how the world works and as guides to problems that need attention.

Merton implicitly left open the question of unit of analysis. If a structure helps satisfy a functional need, then what is the unit having that functional need? Merton dealt with this question in a way most people find intuitively appealing. Merton thought that every social unit had functional needs, and the things one unit did to satisfy its own functional needs may hamper another unit in its effort to satisfy functional needs. Merton even identified desirable consequences of what might otherwise be undesirable systemic arrangements. As an illustration, he noted that corrupt political machines typically dispensed some benefits for people in need.

Merton's example introduces what organizational theorists have come to refer to as "coupling." Tight coupling involves high levels of communication between units, high levels of resource interdependence (connection based on input/output flow), ties based on relative positioning in the same chain of command, a strong sense of common fate, and a commitment to common values and objectives. Weak coupling is the opposite. Although not explicit about this, Merton treated society as a weakly coupled system. As a consequence of weak coupling, relatively isolated or autonomous units can focus on provincial goals and pursue their own (provincial) goal-related activity with comparatively little concern either for what they contribute to the broader system or how their actions might inadvertently generate costs for others units (i.e., what economists call "externalized costs"). It is important to recognize that Merton developed his particular approach to structural–functionalism because he tended to regard society as a weakly coupled system.

Parsons understood society differently. And for theorists who are heavily involved in discussion of structural–functionalism, this is an important point. Parsons implicitly views society as a tightly coupled system. In fact, for society to be functional instead of dysfunctional, one requisite is integration, or the development of unifying patterns of relationships tethering the different parts of the system together—in a phrase, tight coupling. When coupling is tight, units are not isolated or autonomous. There are few provincial goals because local units define their particular goals in obvious connection with and in clear support of the wider whole. Accountability is in terms of what the local unit contributes to the wider whole, and part of the calculus of contribution is to consider the drag one unit places on other units. Consciousness of externalized costs is high, and local units are prevented from adopting practices that generate high levels of externalized costs.

Stated as a general principle, these ideas can be applied either to organizations or to societies, and can be used to explain either the relative proliferation or the relative absence of provincial objectives that distract attention from broader objectives.

The Principle of Systemic Coupling: *Other things being equal, the more tightly coupled units are (the more communication between units, the more resource interdependence, the more meaningful the connection in a chain of command, the stronger the sense of common fate, and the higher the commitment to common values) and the more clearly defined common objectives are, then the less likely common objectives are to be supplanted by provincial ones and the more effective the pursuit of shared objectives will be.*

This takes the fundamental "disagreements" between Parsons and Merton and puts them in their proper place within a science framework. Parsons and Merton wrote theoretical characterizations that diverged somewhat. Merton looked at cases that made him aware of how often provincial interests could sideline societal concerns. Local political corruption was one of his more vivid illustrations. Parsons, by contrast, looked at instances that made him appreciate how much societal needs, commonly shared values, and government authority could override provincial concerns. The spread of universal compulsory education was an important example in Parsons's view. But presuming that either Parsons or Merton was right about coupling and the other was wrong doesn't really resolve anything. Resolution will come when we recognize the strength/intensity of coupling as a variable and develop a principle to help us explain why coupling is relatively strong in some cases and relatively weak in others. When we have done that, we will have come one step closer to Comte's vision of a body of social science principles we can use.

Parsons, for his part, never denied that the way the social world was currently structured had negative consequences. Nor was he blind to the fact that social entities such as government units can be hijacked to serve special interests. He knew those things happened. His question was really: Why don't those with power always succeed in hijacking private organizations or government agencies to serve their special interests? How is it that there are times when change does seem to work to the general benefit of a society and its members? Parsons believed that answering these questions would lead to discoveries that could be used constructively to shape a better world. The Achilles' heel of structural–functionalism has been this assumption that feedback processes will work well to promote system improvement. Sometimes things turn out that way and sometimes they do not. And this needs to be better understood.

THE FOUR FUNCTION SCHEME

Parsons's mature theory took shape in what became known as the "four function scheme." As with a good deal of sociological theory, you have to read a lot of confusing material to piece together what he was actually saying. But the rudimentary ideas are easy enough to see and can be summarized in straightforward terms.

Parsons is best understood as a great synthesizer. He began his career by working for a decade on a book integrating Durkheim, Weber, Pareto, and the British economist Marshall. It was this book, *The Structure of Social Action* (1937), that inaugurated Parsons's career effort to build a comprehensive structural–functional synthesis out of earlier sociological theories.[5] For the next forty years, Parsons labored to develop a structural–functional framework for describing how societies work.

Parsons's structural–functional framework really took shape after publication of *The Social System*. Parsons's starting point for analysis of "structure" was to use Weberian ideal-typing as an analytical technique guided by Weber's preoccupation with the importance of societal value differences. For Parsons, the importance of structure, which for him meant the relationships and understandings and regulatory controls that commit us to a pattern of behavior, was that it reflected "functional" solutions to challenges social systems face. Parsons applied the ideas he acquired from Weber by adopting Durkheim's preoccupation with integration as a system function and drawing from Pareto to conceive of structural solutions (à la Weber) to functional problems (à la Durkheim) as being fine-tuned through equilibrium feedback mechanisms (à la Pareto).

Parsons's explanatory approach took on more clarity over time, as he came to appreciate how most human activity was directed by one of four component elements of social structure: values, norms, collectivities, and roles. Parsons maintained that these four elements of social structure changed over time to better meet one of four social system needs: latent pattern maintenance (basic value agreement), integration (the development of a stable and coherent pattern of unifying relations tethering people together), goal attainment (setting collective priorities and deciding how to meet those priorities), and adaptation (mobilizing resources and marshaling effort for the pursuit of collective priorities).

Faced with the same four basic social-system challenges, Parsons believed every society would more or less blunder along in the direction of solutions having some fundamental similarities. In other words, societies typically follow the same general evolutionary path. The four types of evolutionary change he predicted were value generalization (deciding what the truly important core values are), inclusion (moving toward norms that apply to people more uniformly—more nearly one set of rules for men and women, for example), structural differentiation (more structural autonomy and functional separation for organizational subunits), and role upgrading (better training for everyone). This evolutionary scheme is outlined in one of his easier books to read, *Societies, Evolutionary and Comparative Perspectives*, published in 1966,[6] and it is developed in more detail in Parsons and Platt, *The American University*, released in 1973.[7]

This is how Parsons integrated key ideas from Weber (especially the primacy of values, exemplified by the shift toward a more rational society in which professionals tend to be governed by a sense of responsibility to clients, to their professions, and to the society at large), with key ideas from Durkheim (especially the idea of social structure, in the form of attachments and beliefs, evolving to better meet system needs under changing circumstances), and with ideas from Pareto (especially Pareto's analysis of societies as systems in which equilibrating processes can be observed). People think Parsons's theory is difficult to understand, but it is not. Parsons was always interested in *big* patterns of change, such as the industrial revolution, the democratic revolution, and the educational revolution. He wondered why these big patterns of change occurred when and how they did. He looked for explanations in (macro-)societal–level processes rather than in face-to-face interaction. He tried to be aware of vested interests, but he assumed the hold of special interests could be eroded to bring about change in the best interest of society at large.

GETTING PRACTICAL ABOUT "FUNCTIONAL" OUTCOMES

The optimism captured in the Structural–Functionalist Axiom is rejected by many, especially those informed by Marx, who are justifiably suspicious of power. This disagreement allows us to identify some central questions that will have to be addressed before sociology can successfully integrate structural–functionalism with conflict theory. Those questions are: What kinds of structural forms tend to either mitigate against or facilitate the hijacking of social institutions by special interests? What do we mean by a system need? How can we recognize when systems needs are being met or are unmet? Under what conditions should we expect feedback mechanisms to work, so that problem-solving structural change results when system needs are poorly met? Conversely, under what conditions should we expect to see the feedback and response system fail? Under what conditions should we expect well-positioned special interests to hijack public organizations and use them for private ends? And conversely, how can commitment to general betterment be maintained in public and private organizations? Conflict theorists really need to ask the same set of questions. Generally speaking, people working in the conflict perspective have been more successful at addressing these questions (discussed in chapter 12). When sociologists have better answers to these questions, we are likely to see an integration of the different theoretical perspectives into a single framework that offers coherent explanations for different outcomes under different circumstances.

STRUCTURAL STRAIN

Parsons was clearly more influenced by Weber's intellectual style than by the style of Durkheim, or for that matter Pareto, Mead, or Marx. What we see in Parsons, as a result, is a career-long exuberance for generating typologies rather than explanatory principles. But the explanatory insight Parsons does develop speaks to some of the most fundamental issues facing society. Parsons's theory calls attention to what he called structural strain, or inconsistency among the various elements of social structure.

At the time Parsons was beginning his work, the Civil Rights Movement was not visible enough to have much public recognition in the mainstream press. Most white Americans did not expect much change, but Parsons did. His theory brought him to expect and to welcome change. Parsons and the other structural–functionalists were adamant in pointing to the fact that American values stressing equality of opportunity did not square with exclusion from opportunity on the basis of race. They were painfully aware of the contradiction between American values of equality of opportunity and the reality of discriminatory practices in American society at that time. There was, for example, widespread use of "restrictive covenants" on land titles. Restrictive covenants said that if you owned a home in a neighborhood reserved for whites you could not sell that home to an African American or an Asian American. Discrimination in college admissions and employment was also rampant. Structural–functionalists reasoned that serious structural strain, that is, dramatic inconsistency between values and reality, had to be relieved through structural change. Either the values have to change or practices have to be modified. Moreover, Parsons was convinced that when change came about as a result of structural strain, values normally won. Practices change to conform to values rather than the other way around. For this reason, the long-run outcome of the Civil Rights Movement was never in doubt for structural–functionalists. When many people were saying "you can't fight city hall or the statehouse," the structural–functionalists were saying "state policies that trample on deeply held values cannot last." This was the interpretation in Gunnar Myrdal's 1944 book *An American Dilemma.*[8] Although there is not a Nobel Prize in sociology yet, Myrdal, the second sociologist to win a Nobel Prize, shared the award for economics in 1974. (Jane Addams had won a Nobel Peace Prize some years before.) This important structural–functional idea about values and reality can be captured as the Principle of Structural Strain.

Principle of Structural Strain: *Other things being equal, the greater the awareness of disparity between values and common patterns of behavior, the more likely patterns of behavior are to change in the direction of greater consistency with core social values.*

The centrality of this principle in Parsons's work is attested to by the fact that all of Parsons's treatments of institutions (education, family, religion, law, mechanisms for monitoring professional ethics) emphasize the role institutions play in inculcating and defending core values. Parsons and Platt's *The American University* provides a good illustration.

CONTRASTING STRUCTURAL–FUNCTIONALISM AND CONFLICT THEORY AT A METATHEORETICAL LEVEL

An analysis of the Enron debacle and other instances of unbridled corporate greed and corruption can illustrate the basic metatheoretical differences between structural–functionalism and conflict theory. Doing so is useful, because it highlights some of the questions we need to address in order to make more theoretical progress.

The Enron scandal had to do with the use of bookkeeping and reporting practices that were used to make Enron look much more profitable and secure than it really was. Armed with misleading information, individual investors and mutual funds and pension plans paid a premium price to buy Enron stock, thinking it was a low-risk and high-return asset. Executives were rewarded for their creative accounting because it made the company look good. But when the truth came out, the corporation collapsed, auditors got in trouble for having given the company's financial records a clean bill of health, and government regulators were criticized for not uncovering the problem earlier. This all leads to a nice test question. Is the society really evolving, becoming stronger and better able to meet challenges, if the system operates in a way that retirees lose their pensions and investors lose their confidence?

There is a case to be made for (and also a case to be made against) a structural–functionalist interpretation that things are getting better. Here is the case for a structural–functional interpretation: We are now much better off than we were in the 1920s, when there were very few regulatory protections for people. The stock market crash of 1929 and the Great Depression of the 1930s made it clear that excesses had to be controlled. The

Securities and Exchange Commission and other regulatory agencies were created to offer some oversight and constrain excesses, and universities began doing more to train business people in their fiduciary responsibilities. After a long period of relatively smooth going, regulatory enforcement did get sloppy and a "greed is good" mentality did find somewhat more expression in business schools. However, (a) the sloppy enforcement of the 1990s was better than the no rules environment of the 1890s and (b) the "profit is good" vocabulary of the 1990s was better than the "if it isn't nailed down it is mine and if I can pry it loose it isn't nailed down" attitude of 1890s robber barons. Most people in most corporations were doing their jobs appropriately in the 1990s. This seems to show that the long-term trend is away from special interests being able to hijack the system. Now may well be the right time to ratchet up regulation and put energy into socializing future professionals to be more vigilant about protecting the public interest, but from a structural–functionalist point of view we are much better off than we were in 1929, because of the evolution that has occurred since. That evolution finds society better able, rather than less able, to meet challenges. Thus there seems to be some evolutionary improvement in "the system."

There is also a case to be made for a conflict interpretation that things are getting worse: The few times people are caught, the penalty is insignificant in relationship with the damage done. Tightened enforcement lasts only as long as public attention is focused on the issue. Even those organizations that are ostensibly devoted to defense of the public interest against special interests seem themselves to be transformed into special interests over time. Once auditors and/or regulators are co-opted, the situation may be worse than ever, because the existence of auditors and regulators creates an aura of legitimacy to whatever is happening. And, ultimately, every organization develops interests of its own and tends to forget the wider collective interest of the general public.[9] Finally, time may be running out. Resource depletion, pollution, and other problems are overtaking us. So even if we are fixing problems a little bit, we may not be fixing them fast enough to do any good.

The challenge sociologists face is to move beyond axiomatic statements such as "people work to promote the collective good" or "people work to protect their own self-interest" and begin articulating some principles about the conditions under which public interest will trump special interests and, conversely, the conditions under which powerful interest groups will be able to hijack public or private organizations, and perhaps even government agencies, and use them for personal ends. Our first step is to acknowledge the axiomatic assumptions being made. The implicit promise of science is that we can make progress by advancing principles that explain and predict variation.

RECAP

Structural–functionalism is often mischaracterized as opposing change. Quite the opposite is true. It is based on the premise that change is necessary (and desirable) to adapt to shifting circumstances. So structural–functionalism as a theoretical framework is definitely not antichange.

Structural–functionalists emphasize the importance of doing things in ways that are consistent with our most important values. This often means changing the way the society operates, so structural–functionalism is definitely not inherently pro–status quo. Structural–functionalists tend to assume that change works toward rather than away from the greater collective good. In certain instances, this seems to be the case, and in other instances it seems not to be the case. Consequently, structural–functionalists need to do more to understand how feedback and change processes work, in order to explain why outcomes are (or certainly seem to be) sometimes detrimental rather than beneficial. Robert Merton's more open treatment of functions (positive and negative, intended and unintended, considering all units and not just the society as a whole) can provide a useful conceptual tool as we try to better understand how countervailing pressures and tendencies come to be resolved in a complex world. Talcott Parsons performed an amazing intellectual feat by integrating the ideas of Weber, Durkheim, and Pareto. And while his conceptual framework is cumbersome, it is not difficult to understand in its broad outline. Parsons was also methodologically creative, as illustrated by his examination of social roles for triangulating on qualitative differences in societal values.

NOTES

1. Vilfredo Pareto, *The Transformation of Democracy* (New Brunswick, N.J.: Transaction, 1984).
2. Barbara Heyl, "The Harvard 'Pareto Circle,'" *Journal of the History of the Behavioral Sciences* 4, no. 4 (October 1968): 316–34.

3. Talcott Parsons, *The Social System* (New York: Free Press, 1951).

4. Robert K. Merton, *Social Theory and Social Structure* (Glencoe, Ill.: Free Press, 1968).

5. Talcott Parsons, *The Structure of Social Action* (New York: McGraw-Hill, 1937).

6. Talcott Parsons, *Societies: Evolutionary and Comparative Perspectives* (Englewood Cliffs, N.J.: Prentice-Hall, 1966).

7. Talcott Parsons and Gerald Platt, *The American University* (Cambridge, Mass.: Harvard University Press, 1973).

8. Gunnar Myrdal, *An American Dilemma* (New York: Harper & Row, 1944).

9. Philip Selznick, *TVA and the Grass Roots* (Berkeley: University of California Press, 1949).

SOME TERMS TO KNOW

Stable Equilibrium. The tendency of a system to return to its original state, as when increasing demand generates higher prices and demand then softens (returning to its original point) in response to higher prices.

Moving Equilibrium. The tendency of a system to move to a new equilibrium point, as when high profits encourage new research, resulting in breakthroughs that lead in turn to reduced prices and even higher demand at a new supply/demand equilibrium point.

Structural Strain. Inconsistency among the various elements of social structure.

REVIEW OF AXIOMS AND PRINCIPLES

Form Follows Function Axiom: *Form follows function in the sense that widespread patterns of structural change emerge as systemic responses to meet new needs or correct for poor performance in the face of old needs.*

The Principle of Systemic Coupling: *Other things being equal, the more tightly coupled units are (the more communication between units, the more resource interdependence, the more meaningful the connection in a chain of command, the stronger the sense of common fate, and the higher the commitment to common values) and the more clearly defined common objec-*

tives are, then the less likely common objectives are to be supplanted by provincial ones and the more effective the pursuit of shared objectives will be.

Principle of Structural Strain: *Other things being equal, the greater the awareness of disparity between values and common patterns of behavior, the more likely patterns of behavior are to change in the direction of greater consistency with core social values.*

CHAPTER REVIEW TEST

Check your answers against the key in the back of the book. If you get any wrong, reread chapter 11, thinking about it as you go, before moving on to chapter 12.

1. It is often said that form follows function. What does that mean?

2. Parsons believed that social change followed an evolutionary progression. That is, over the long course of time, structural change tends to move in predictable directions. What directions did he think change tended to move in, over the long course of time?

3. What is one of the contributions to structural–functionalism that Robert K. Merton is most often remembered for?

APPLICATION EXERCISE

In recent years, many states have imposed testing requirements for high school graduation. How are we to make sense of this? Do you think it is better understood as a protection for the society or as a protection for some special-interest group? Setting aside the interests that individual people might have in this issue, does the society as a social whole have any interest in it? Jot down a few notes indicating what you think those interests might be, focusing on what you regard as "societal interests" that transcend individual interests. Do you think there is a process that allows a society to define its societal interests? If so, what do you think that process is? How well do you think it works?

12

CONFLICT THEORY

Always Ask Who Benefits

Structural–functionalist ideas were being discussed at Harvard University and elsewhere throughout the 1930s and 1940s, but did not emerge as a clearly articulated theoretical paradigm until the early 1950s. As that was happening, many people rejected the metatheoretical assumptions that structural–functionalists tended to make about society being a system organized to progressively redesign itself for the common good. Their views eventually coalesced into conflict theory as a recognizable intellectual framework. Call the critics pessimists, or call them realists. What matters is they made different metatheoretical assumptions than those of the structural–functionalists. Conflict theorists tended to assume that power corrupts and that the institutions of society develop in ways that are intended to keep the rich and the poor in their respective places. As a result, conflict theorists generally focus on sensitizing concepts such as class, vested interests, stratification, and power. By the late 1950s, a conflict paradigm was successfully challenging the intellectual hegemony of structural–functionalism in sociology.

CONFLICT'S REJECTION OF
STRUCTURAL–FUNCTIONALIST METATHEORY

To understand conflict theory, one has to appreciate its basic metatheoretical rejection of the structural–functionalist position that was preeminent in American sociology by 1955. From outside the discipline in 1955, sociological theory could easily have appeared to be structural–functionalism. But strong axiomatic objections were stirring, and two alternative meta-theoretical perspectives quickly coalesced into theoretical frameworks having explanatory power. These were conflict theory (discussed in this chapter) and, slightly later, symbolic interactionism (discussed in chapter 13).

The conflict perspective emphasizes the self-serving nature of powerful people and calls into question whether any reform-oriented structural change brokered by people in positions of power will be genuine or meaningful. Instead, conflict theorists tend to suspect that change brokered by people in power will always be designed to protect and extend the interests of those who are already advantaged. While structural–functionalists are convinced that greed can and should be curbed, for the good of society, by transmitting altruistic values through education, conflict theorists tend to think that any altruism on the part of the powerful is merely superficial.

Structure Inequality Axiom: *The social structural arrangements that evolve and survive tend to be those that protect the interests of more powerful people at the expense of less powerful people.*

The disagreement between conflict theorists and structural–functionalists will only be resolved when we have principles stipulating when and how altruistic values will subordinate self-interest. Conflict theorists have already made some significant progress in developing explanatory principles that help us understand how conflict actually unfolds in the real world. In this chapter, we will review how the conflict framework assumed some of its current form.

UNMASKING OF THE POWER ELITE BY REDISCOVERING MARX

American sociology's rediscovery of Marx began with the urban ethnography of Robert Lynd and Helen Merrell Lynd. They spent several years studying Muncie, Indiana. In the 1920s, America was rapidly urbanizing, and church leaders in Muncie were concerned about the decline of church attendance and the spread of urban-style social problems. A consortium of churches hired a husband and wife team of sociologists to conduct a study. The goal was to gauge the problem and suggest ways of getting people back to church.

The Lynds spent several years interviewing people and conducting surveys in and around Muncie. One of their principal discoveries was exactly what readers of Marx had anticipated. Class matters. The businesspeople of Muncie made most of the important decisions in government and in civic circles, as well as in the economy. While the Lynds did provide Muncie's religious leaders with useful information about declining church attendance, their lasting sociological contribution was to improve our understanding of class in the United States.[1]

A revealing set of community studies that followed in the tradition of *Middletown* all showed that businesspeople have enormous political and civic as well as economic clout. Studies of movers and shakers have confirmed this, discovering what C. Wright Mills aptly described "the power elite" in his 1956 book by that title.[2] William Domhoff is one of many people to try to discover how the power elite exerts control over local, state, and national government, and over organizations of every kind, from behind the scenes. In his 1974 book, *The Bohemian Grove and Other Retreats*, Domhoff describes how private social clubs can serve as meeting grounds for the rich, enabling them to develop a sense of group feeling and chart strategies for promoting shared interests.[3] One of the interesting offshoots of the power elite literature charts interlocking directorates. The boards of directors of power-wielding organizations such as banks, big corporations, and high-profile civic groups often have overlapping membership. This gives some objective reality to the idea of a truly *ruling*, and not simply rich, "ruling class." Working together on boards of directors of corporations and nonprofit organizations, and sitting on advisory panels for government, a few individuals can communicate with each other and have profound influence. Needless to say, those well-connected individuals come from the top of the society and not the bottom, and their positions give them real voice. They are not the "silent majority." Nor are they the "voiceless underclass."

Of course, there is significant variation from place to place. A power elite seems to hold almost monolithic power in some times and places, such as in cities with only a few industries that are tightly controlled by a small number of people from a few interrelated families. Where education and human capital are scarce, as in Atlanta during the 1940s and early 1950s, when Floyd Hunter wrote *Community Power Structure* (1953), it is hard for voices of dissent to be heard.[4] Political power and civic influence seem to be more pluralistic in cities where there are many industries, where a diverse array of people are less thoroughly interconnected with each other, and where education and human capital are relatively abundant and widely dispersed, as Robert Dahl found in New Haven when he wrote *Who Governs?* in 1961.[5] The studies by Hunter and Dahl, with their varied findings, suggest an explanatory principle.

Pluralist Governance Principle: *Other things being equal, the more diverse economic activity and organized social life are, the more broadly distributed control over economic activity and organized social life is, the higher the level and broader the distribution of education and other forms of human capital, and the more diverse and open are channels of public communication, then the greater the number and broader the diversity of interest groups that will have the ability to influence the agendas of civic, government, and community organizations and the more pluralistic governance will be.*

Although some structural–functionalists blindly assume that the normal operation of power yields changes that serve the collective good, and some conflict theorists blindly assume that the normal operation of power yields changes that foster greater exploitation by those in power, the empirical truth seems to be that both descriptions are more or less accurate, but for different times and places. The social science challenge is to understand how special interests make themselves felt in corridors of power (a question the conflict framework is well positioned to help us answer), and conversely, how their grip over the public arena can be broken (a question the structural–functionalist framework may be positioned to help us answer).

Moving forward in this respect has meant moving beyond Marx. When Marx laid out the basic theoretical premises of conflict theory in the mid-nineteenth century, the era of "Big Business" was only beginning. That was before anything that we would recognize as a modern industrial economy had developed anywhere. It was before cars, before department stores, before any antitrust legislation, and before the establishment of the Federal Reserve Board. It was a full century before the World Bank and the International Monetary Fund. Aware of all the historical developments postdating Marx's description of early industrial capitalism, Marxian writers have (since the Lynds) tried to analyze current conditions from the vantage point of Marx's theoretical framework, but as they think he would be applying the framework if he were alive today. Making Marx's ideas more contemporary has, in fact, been the single biggest preoccupation of people who identify themselves as working within the conflict tradition.

NEO-MARXIST ANALYSIS OF CLASS

For conflict theorists informed by a Marxian conceptual framework, all questions ultimately return to descriptions of the class structure. But modern class structure is not as simple as Marx imagined it would be when he and Engels wrote *The Communist Manifesto* in 1848.[6] Marx observed that owners and workers were fundamentally different in almost every respect in early capitalist society. And he was convinced that these differences would grow more pronounced as capitalism matured. He predicted that owners would have total workplace authority and wage earners would have no workplace authority at all. In an age of automation, Marx thought that the jobs of most wage earners would be deskilled over time, and that the wages of employees could then be driven down to a starvation level.

But contemporary reality is somewhat different. For one thing, many wage earners actually have a lot of job authority. If we look at the economy as a whole, some of the largest occupational categories (e.g., managers and foreman) fall into the "ambiguous" class position of being employees themselves, yet having supervisory authority. These people are typically accorded more respect, higher wages, and better benefits than other workers. Nevertheless, they are still what Marx would regard as "wage slaves" who have to sell their labor in order to survive. Furthermore, the human capital of working people has grown rather than shriveled as a consequence of technological change. While it is true that some old crafts have largely disappeared, a technology-based economy requires people with more skill rather than less. To make a summary comment, today's typical worker is simply not in the dire position in which Marx anticipated capitalism would deposit all workers with the passage of time.

All of these factors combine to create a contemporary class structure in which many people, perhaps the majority of workers in the United States, are in fact wage earners who share some of the characteristics Marx associated with being a member of the capitalist class. As Erik Wright pointed out in his 1978 book, *Class, Crisis, and the State,* this puts people in "ambig-uous" class positions where their class interests can seem somewhat murky and conflicted.[7] Wright and other conflict theorists wonder what it will mean if most people come to feel that they actually have one foot in each of the main classes Marx described. The answer seems pretty ob-vious to most sociologists. Class ambiguity discourages class conflict by mitigating against polarizing class consciousness.

Conflict theorists have also developed deep appreciation for the impor-tant and pervasive ways in which class manifests itself through control of knowledge and manners, apart from control of financial resources and means of production. Bourdieu and Passeron write about "culture capi-tal," or manners and knowledge that signal one's right to be treated as a person of special worth.[8] Having "culture capital" in the form of impres-sive knowledge and preferred manners also helps people build "social capital," or useful contacts and network connections expanding one's scope of opportunity.

One especially interesting aspect of this work is the concept of "sym-bolic violence." Just as the people with culture capital tend to feel entitled to the good things in life, those people who lack much of what is ap-proved as standard culture capital tend to feel that they are undeserving. Getting poor people to blame themselves for the fact that they have few advantages in life constitutes "symbolic violence," to the degree that it directs the substantial psychological costs of poverty inward in the form of self-loathing and thereby increases the likelihood of continued failure.

CONFLICT THEORIES OF THE STATE

Among the conflict theorists interested in seats of political power, some of the most interesting discussion has swirled around attempts to under-stand the role of the modern state. Nicos Poulantzas is one of many peo-ple who ask what Marx might have said about the role of the state if Marx were alive today. Poulantzas, in his 1978 book, *State, Power, and Socialism,* argues that Marx would reject simpleminded notions that the state is con-trolled by individual capitalists. Instead, Poulantzas's Marxian view is that the state functions as a sort of capitalist clearing house, promoting the general interests of business without necessarily supporting every sin-gle vested interest of every single business owner.[9] What happens, for ex-ample, when oil companies want high gas prices that increase their profits, but at the same time, auto manufacturers would prefer low gas prices so they can sell more SUVs? And of course, this begs the question of international capital. Are the interests of Toyota and Honda, known best for reliable economy cars, the same as the interests of GM and Ford, generally known for more powerful but less efficient vehicles? Conflict theorists struggle with questions such as this.

That struggle often comes back to the question posed by Poulantzas. How can we make sense of a collective interest of those who are economically powerful? Poulantzas and most other conflict theorists believe that the ruling class as a whole, as distinguished from individual people with wealth or power, has some collective interests. This is highly relevant if we think of a power elite hijacking control of the government for its own interests. Which interests are we talking about? Are we talking about the interests of those few who happen to be in momentary control? Or are we talking about the interests of some broader class or grouping? What can we say about the processing through which special interests and common public interests gain definition and vie for influence?

The flip side of this equation, explored by general conflict theorists, concerns government's efforts to maintain its legitimacy in the eyes of common people. To maintain legitimacy, governments can be expected to utilize propaganda tactics to deflect blame for any problems toward internal opposition or external enemies. Government might also be called on to provide safety net protections and maintain official mechanisms for adjudication of grievances. Gurtov and Maghroori capture these insights in their 1984 book, *Roots of Failure: United States Foreign Policy in the Third World,* in which they attribute the fall of governments to the loss of legitimacy that comes from a widespread perception that the interests of average people are ill-served by those in power.[10]

Principle of Legitimate Authority: *Other things being equal, authority tends to be perceived as legitimate to the degree that (a) protection of rights and provision of services are thought to be reliable, (b) adjudication of grievances by administrative agents is seen as fair, and (c) ideology and information are skillfully used to deflect blame in the direction of internal opposition or external enemies.*

Correlating to this is the recognition that domestic crises often come to a head after long periods of fiscal overextension (deficit spending) and/or projection of military power.[11]

GENERAL CONFLICT THEORY

Most conflict theorists focus on traditional Marxian concerns. These include (a) inequality between business owners and wage earners, (b) control of government and manipulation of media and ideology to protect the interests of business owners, and (c) class conflict. There are, however, conflict theorists who have tried to develop more general frameworks for studying conflict of all kinds. This general conflict tradition started in Germany with Georg Simmel, who was a friend of Max Weber's and one of the original founders of the German Sociological Society. As we noted earlier, Simmel was fascinated by conflict as a category of phenomena that is generic and pervasive in everyday life. One of his great insights is that conflict between groups tends to lead to increased cohesion within groups.

Simmel, like his friend Max Weber, was ever alert to the ubiquitous nature of conflict, and he was convinced that sociology needed to broaden its focus beyond Marx's preoccupation with societal change stemming from the revolutionary clash of business owners and wage earners. Weber's analytical separation of (economic) *class* from (social) *status* and (political) *power* is evidence of an approach to conflict that is much broader than that of Marx. And Simmel's concern for conflict in ordinary, day-to-day human interaction is broader still. Among other things, the positive consequences of conflict need to be appreciated, a point developed in Lewis Coser's *The Functions of Social Conflict* (1956).[12] Conflict, Simmel recognized, has all sorts of positive consequences, not the least of which is alerting people when something is not working well and needs to be addressed.

The German intellectual interest in conflict in all its many forms crystallized in Ralf Dahrendorf's *Class and Class Conflict in Industrial Society* (1959).[13] Dahrendorf focused on the fact that relationships between people with different levels of organizational authority are inherently conflict ridden. His theory of conflict is as revealing as it is elegant in its simplicity. Dahrendorf said the following:

1. Conflict tends to occur between those who have organizational authority and those who do not.
2. Conflict is orchestrated into group action more rapidly: (a) if grievance procedures exist and there is a history of using them, (b) if people at the same authority level are able to communicate with one an-

other, (c) if a leadership cadre exists among those at subordinate levels of authority, (d) if ideologies pinpoint rather than obscure lines of division between those with and without authority, (e) when the range of similarities within authority levels and differences between authority levels are greatest, and (f) where ties across authority levels are limited in number. (Note the incorporation of Marx's fundamental insight about intergroup antagonism, reviewed in chapter 7.)

3. The more often conflict is played out, then the less likely it is to turn violent and the more likely it is to lead to progressive rather than punctuated change.

4. When conflict is played out, it eventually leads to structural change relieving old pressures, though it often creates the conditions under which new ones will develop.

Dahrendorf's scheme has the beauty of being applicable to any situation where there are authority differences built into organizational roles. But his analysis does rest on an assumption.

Corruption of Power Axiom: *The powerful do not loosen the grip of exploitation without being pressed to.*

The existence of authority differences gives rise to the possibility of abuse or perceived abuse of power, and when conflict arises, structural change aimed at reducing friction becomes more likely. Hence, Dahrendorf would say that in every organization there are ways for people in authority to get special benefits. Over time, this generates resentment and conflict. The more resentment that is generated and the more that conflict erupts, then the more likely structural change becomes. Typically, change brought about in this way will correct some problems. But over time, new people in positions of authority will find their own path through which to benefit, and resentment and conflict will follow. Interestingly, conflict is more likely to turn violent if it is episodic rather than chronic, and when it occurs outside of an arena with rules and procedures.

Conflict theorists as diverse as Marx and Dahrendorf would agree on a set of fundamental premises that can be expressed in two predictive principles.

Principle of Intergroup Conflict: *Other things being equal, (a) the more pronounced intergroup antagonism becomes, (b) the more historical/sym-*

bolic unity there is within each group and the more historical/symbolic division there is between groups, and (c) the more communication there is within groups and the less communication there is between groups, then the more likely intergroup antagonism is to lead to conflict.

Principle of Violent Conflict: *Other things being equal, the more recurrent and procedurally regulated conflict is, the less likely it is to turn violent.*

One of the restrictions of Dahrendorf's approach and the approach of many other conflict theorists is that they explicitly focus on situations in which conflict occurs along a fault line defined by differences in wealth or power. However, if we use experience as a guide, we know that conflict also occurs among peers or between groups who are at the same level of organizational power or economic wealth. Theodore Caplow, in his 1968 book, *Two Against One: Coalitions in Triads*, builds upon Simmel's basic insights to explore how conflict dynamics change as soon as an association of people, such as a family or a collection of friends, grows from two individuals (a dyad) to three individuals (a triad).[14] Instantly, the possibilities for coalition formation make themselves apparent. And coalitions can shift over time.

DEPENDENCY AND WORLD SYSTEM THEORY

One feature of conflict theory that has special appeal is its applicability to different units of analysis. At one extreme, Caplow examines coalition formation within triads, groups of three people, for example, a parent and two children. At the other extreme, Andre Gunder Frank, in his 1967 *Capitalism and Underdevelopment in Latin America*, considers the dependence that he says elites in poor nations develop on rich nations,[15] and Immanuel Wallerstein, in his *The Modern World System*, examines the flow of events that tie the fate of nations producing resources (lumber, sugar, cotton, minerals, and fuel producers) to manufacturing countries in a "world system."[16] Both "dependency" theorists and "world system" theorists try to explain why some countries are relatively rich and others are relatively poor. They generally perceive that relationships of dependence insure that the wealth of the Third World will slowly gravitate into the banks of the industrial West, where those profits will be used to bolster the continued development of the most powerful countries rather than the relatively impoverished lands from which profits were generated. Similar ideas have been used to point toward a kind of "internal colonialism" in which the financial resources of poor rural or poor urban areas end up being siphoned out of those communities rather than invested locally, opening up questions being explored by sociologists in Latin America, including ex-sociology professor Fernando Cardoso, the inflation-fighting president of Brazil (1994–2002), in his 2001 book, *Charting a New Course: The Politics of Globalization and Social Transformation.*[17] But the conclusions these theorists reach are still controversial and contested among academics. Theorists are busy grappling with these questions, as the current debate over neoliberalism and globalization attests.

A CONCRETE POINT OF DEPARTURE BETWEEN PARADIGMS

Having a coherent sense of sociology as a discipline requires being able to make sense of the ways different paradigms inform our understanding of the world. Education provides a concrete point of departure for understanding what conflict theory and structural–functionalism have in common and how they differ. Both paradigms assume the existence of institutionalized features of society that are bigger than any individual and have enormous consequences. To use a concrete illustration, people working in both paradigms assume that industrial societies mobilize collective resources (taxes, for example) and commit those resources to schools that are monitored and controlled to some degree by government. People employing both paradigms work with the common presumption that school curricula are designed to achieve some planned purpose extending beyond the wishes of a particular group of students and their parents. The curriculum is more or less imposed on students by school systems. It is widely understood that most students have little recourse but to go along with "the system," and that each student's future opportunities as well as present experience are shaped by the nature of educational institutions and the curricular and delivery decisions those institutions make.

At this point, the similarity between conflict theory and structural–functionalism ends. As noted at the conclusion of the last chapter, structural–functionalists regard educational institutions as having emerged and undergone steady change oriented to promote the common good. Schools are seen by structural–functionalists as imparting technical knowledge, cultural graces, and democratic civility. They are viewed as promoting altruism as a social value, so that well-educated students will mature into adults working in the common interest. But from a conflict perspective, schools are viewed as instruments for solidifying the class structure, insuring that the children of rich and powerful people will themselves be helped along on the road to their own wealth and power, and that the children of lower-income workers are molded into compliant followers who will settle for whatever they are given.[18]

Conflict theory and structural–functional theory lead us to expect different things. It is good that we be alert to both scenarios because both outcomes are possible. But if our goal in science is to explain variation, our ultimate task as theorists will be to discover principles that allow for the possibility of both outcomes and help us understand why different outcomes come to pass in different cases.

RECAP

Conflict theory is not a tightly integrated body of thought. Instead, it consists of a wide-ranging collection of works applying the same set of metatheoretical assumptions in different settings. Most work in the conflict tradition seeks to reveal inequality, to explain how inequality is created and maintained, and to understand its consequences. Research in this tradition has fundamentally transformed our understanding of the social world by revealing just how deeply rooted inequality is and how destructive it can be. The conflict tradition is informed by Marx's critique of the nineteenth-century class situation. But it is also more. The critique of class and power has been revised in light of developments as they have unfolded with the passage of time. Moreover, conflict in all its forms has been brought under examination, with the result that the perspective has relevance to situations of all kinds.

NOTES

1. Robert Lynd and Helen Merrell Lynd, *Middletown in Transition* (New York: Harcourt Brace, 1937).

2. C. Wright Mills, *The Power Elite* (New York: Oxford University Press, 1956).

3. William Domhoff, *The Bohemian Grove and Other Retreats* (New York: Harper & Row, 1974).

4. Floyd Hunter, *Community Power Structure* (Chapel Hill: University of North Carolina Press, 1953).

5. Robert Dahl, *Who Governs?* (New Haven, Conn.: Yale University Press, 1961).

6. Karl Marx and Friedrich Engels, *The Communist Manifesto* (1848; reprint, Northbrook, Ill.: AMH, 1955).

7. Erik Wright, *Class, Crisis, and the State* (London: New Left, 1978).

8. Pierre Bourdieu and J. Passeron, *Reproduction in Education, Society, and Culture* (Beverly Hills: Sage, 1977).

9. Nicos Poulantzas, *State, Power, and Socialism* (London: New Left, 1979).

10. Melvin Gurtov and Ray Maghroori, *The Roots of Failure: United States Foreign Policy in the Third World* (Westport, Conn.: Greenwood, 1984).

11. Theda Skocpol, *States and Social Revolutions* (New York: Cambridge University Press, 1979).

12. Lewis Coser, *The Functions of Social Conflict* (New York: Free Press, 1956).

13. Ralf Dahrendorf, *Class and Class Conflict in Industrial Society* (Stanford, Calif.: Stanford University Press, 1959).

14. Theodore Caplow, *Two Against One: Coalitions in Triads* (Englewood Cliffs, N.J.: Prentice-Hall, 1986).

15. Andre Gunder Frank, *Capitalism and Underdevelopment in Latin America* (New York: Monthly Review Press, 1967).

16. Immanuel Wallerstein, *The Modern World System*, 2 vols. (New York: Academic, 1974, 1980).

17. Fernando Cardoso, *Charting a New Course: The Politics of Globalization and Social Transformation* (Lanham, Md.: Rowman & Littlefield, 2001).

18. Randall Collins, *The Credential Society* (New York: Academic, 1978).

SOME TERMS TO KNOW

Culture Capital. Ways in which upper-class status manifests itself through control of knowledge and manners.

Social Capital. Useful contacts and network connections that influence one's access to opportunities.

Symbolic Violence. Self-imposed limitations and distress caused by blaming oneself for problems caused by others.

REVIEW OF AXIOMS AND PRINCIPLES

Structure Inequality Axiom: *The social structural arrangements that evolve and survive tend to be those that protect the interests of more powerful people at the expense of less powerful people.*

Corruption of Power Axiom: *The powerful do not loosen the grip of exploitation without being pressed to.*

Pluralist Governance Principle: *Other things being equal, the more diverse economic activity and organized social life are, the more broadly distributed control over economic activity and organized social life is, the higher the level and broader the distribution of education and other forms of human capital, and the more diverse and open are channels of public communication, then the greater the number and broader the diversity of interest groups that will have the ability to influence the agendas of civic, government, and community organizations and the more pluralistic governance will be.*

Principle of Legitimate Authority: *Other things being equal, authority tends to be perceived as legitimate to the degree that (a) protection of rights and provision of services are thought to be reliable, (b) adjudication of grievances by administrative agents is seen as fair, and (c) ideology and information are skillfully used to deflect blame in the direction of internal opposition or external enemies.*

Principle of Intergroup Conflict: *Other things being equal, (a) the more pronounced intergroup antagonism becomes, (b) the more historical/symbolic unity there is within each group and the more historical/symbolic division there is between groups, and (c) the more communication there is within groups and the less communication there is between groups, then the more likely intergroup antagonism is to lead to organized conflict.*

Principle of Violent Conflict: *Other things being equal, the more recurrent and procedurally regulated conflict is, the less likely it is to turn violent.*

CHAPTER REVIEW TEST

Check your answers against the answer key at the end of the book. If you get any wrong, reread chapter 12, thinking about it as you go, before moving on to chapter 13.

1. What are the most common roots of intergroup conflict?

2. When is a local power elite likely to exert the most monolithic control over local government?

3. How many people have to be in a group before we begin to see coalitions form?

APPLICATION EXERCISE

Describe an instance of conflict between peers. This should not be a conflict that just developed yesterday. It should be a conflict that you have had some time to think about and reflect on. Describe the setting. How many people are/were involved? What kinds of people are these (high school friends, college roommates, coworkers, etc.)? Describe the root of the conflict. What caused it to erupt? What changes, if any, came out of the conflict? Do people like each other more or less than they did before? Did understandings change? Have friendship patterns been modified? Have identities or roles or social position changed as a result?

13

SYMBOLIC INTERACTIONISM IN EVERYDAY LIFE

People Make a Difference

Two articles of faith in science are (1) all understanding is provisional (because we assume all "knowledge" can ultimately be improved upon) and (2) those of us who are engaged in the quest for better understanding have to be willing to articulate our provisional (and very flawed) understandings as a part of the process of moving toward a somewhat more realistic and informative body of theory. The rise of theoretical paradigms in sociology illustrates this point very well. The structural–functional paradigm, taken by itself in its 1950s form, was unrealistically optimistic about the benevolence of societal institutions and power brokers. Many sociologists recognized this, and the conflict paradigm emerged as a corrective. Sometime in the future, we will be able to explain when and how special interests are able to hijack government and other social institutions, and we may also learn how institutions can be better protected from hijacking so that the common good can be served. At that point, we will be able to consolidate the conflict and structural–functionalist paradigms into a single and more powerful theoretical framework. A good natural science analogy is the integration of the early-twentieth-century theory of electricity and the early-twentieth-century theory of magnetism to produce a theory of electromagnetism. That took a lot of effort by theorists. It took a lot of years to achieve. But it did eventually happen, and when it did, it marked a major scientific leap forward.

AGENCY

As those contributing to the development of the conflict paradigm were loudly questioning structural–functionalist assumptions about the benevolence of social institutions, another set of voices began to be heard in greater number. Those were people who questioned the implicit assumptions shared by structural–functionalists and conflict theorists, most notably an assumption of structural determinism. People informed by the work of George Herbert Mead assumed that individuals have considerable agency to shape their commitments and redefine shared meaning. The work of many of those interested in agency coalesced into what has come to be known as the symbolic interactionist perspective.

Symbolic interactionists have always regarded both conflict theory and structural–functional theory as overly deterministic, meaning that too little attention is paid to the fact that people can change their situations, among other things by redefining the contours of their social commitments. The determinism of structural–functional theory and conflict theory implies that the beliefs, behavior, and fate of people are all shaped by characteristics of the wider society, characteristics such as institutional arrangements of family and education, the class structure, legal codes, the police enforcement apparatus, and theological teachings of prevalent religions. But interactionists tend to believe that individuals have more "agency" than structural, cultural, and class determinist models would allow.

Symbolic interactionists all recognize that every society has structural features and cultural characteristics, and that the features and characteristics of the society are very important. Each of us is indelibly marked by the kind of society we live in and our location in it. Symbolic interactionists know and appreciate this. Nevertheless, symbolic interactionists stress that cultural and structural determinism is limited in its consequences, that individual people do exercise agency and are able to significantly reshape the social world, or at least that part of the social world that they personally inhabit.[1] In fairness, it is important to recognize that structural functionalists and conflict theorists also recognize that individuals have agency and can reshape the world in which they live. As sociological theory matures, our task is to develop a set of principles that enables us not only to appreciate the importance of both sets of dynamics, but also to understand their interplay in realistic ways.

With their interest in agency, symbolic interactionists tend to employ a special set of sensitizing concepts that only partially overlaps with those used when the other paradigms are being employed. Symbolic interactionists tend to be acutely aware of definition of situation, self-concept, identity, stigma, emotional arousal, peer groups, reference groups, role strain, and role distance. By the early 1960s, symbolic interactionism had coalesced into a paradigm that was broadly recognized by people in the discipline. This intellectual perspective really had its birth at the University of Chicago.

THE CHICAGO SCHOOL OF SYMBOLIC INTERACTION

Interactionists trained at the University of Chicago emphasized that events are fluid. How people define their situations can be altered. Roles can change as a result. Most people need little convincing of this. Marriage illustrates the point quite well. Some marriages are filled with affection, while others are shrouded in hurt and bitterness. Some marriage unions are warm and cuddly, while others are cold and distant. None of this is prescribed by law or ordained by a fate we are powerless to alter. Couples actually shape and forge the particular character of their marriages through their actions and reactions over time. Interactionists watch as marriages once fresh and full of affection come to the point where they hit a Y in the road, when people's actions and reactions either take them on a path of deepening respect and mature affection (the well-aged "fine wines" of marriage) or on a path of mutual abandonment or even contempt (the sour old vinegars of marriage). The fact is, however, that people have agency, so that what we do actually does make a difference, and so that the people in a relationship have some ability to remold and reshape what there is between them, on one condition. The condition is that both people want to reshape their relationship in the same direction, at the same time. It takes two to tango. It takes two people trying to give passion and respect to build a relationship permeated with passion and respect. One person acting alone is just spitting into the wind.[2] Symbolic interaction is *inter*action. Individual action is what is left of interaction when the "inter" has been amputated. Not much fun for those involved in marriages that have taken this turn.

The marriage example reveals a fundamental characteristic of the Chicago school of symbolic interaction. Symbolic interactionists of the Chicago school don't really ask *why* things happen. Their concern is with process, with *how* things happen. This is illustrated nicely in Louis Zurcher's 1983 book, *Social Roles*. In examining the unfolding of events, symbolic interactionists working within the Chicago tradition have found that reactions can be just as important as initial actions. What is subtly communicated is just as important as what is explicitly vocalized. And what is perceived ("definition of situation") is even more important than what is real. Consider an argument among college roommates. Depending on the flow of interaction, the argument can lead to changes everyone can see: one person moving out, for example. The argument can also lead to a fundamental transformation in relationships among the people involved: a change in specific norms about lights-out or music-off hours, changes in the tenor of the relationship reflected in more respect for each other's likes and dislikes (the good citizen approach), or contempt combined with intentional efforts to offend each other's sensitivities and sensibilities.

The dynamic character of everyday life, and the essential hollowness of deterministic models, was brought to life in Chicago interactionist works such as Tamotsu Shibutani's compelling story of a U.S. Army unit during World War II, *The Derelicts of Company K* (1978).[3] This work merits lengthy discussion because it puts deterministic models to a clear test. The pertinent historical factors are as follows. First, the United States was at war with Japan from 1941 to 1945. Second, at the time the war broke out, there were approximately 130,000 people of Japanese ancestry living in the Hawaiian Islands (then an overseas frontier territory that would not become a state until 1959), while another 130,000 people of Japanese ancestry were living on the mainland, mostly along the West Coast, in places such as Seattle, Los Angeles, and California's Central Valley. Of these Japanese Americans, about half were citizens, because they were born in the United States. The remainder were all noncitizens, because at that time U.S. race-based laws prohibited immigrants from Asia and Africa from becoming naturalized citizens. Third, the U.S. government forced most of the mainland people of Japanese ancestry into what the government usually called "relocation camps," located in remote areas. These were in fact concentration camps (although they were nothing like the Nazi death camps people commonly think of when the term "concentration camp" is used). Fourth, a high proportion of young male U.S. citizens of Japanese ancestry volunteered for the army or were conscripted into the army, and most of them were sent off having been clearly told by their families that they needed to fight bravely for the United States to earn the trust of other Americans.

Fifth, at the time, the U.S. Army was racially segregated, and most Japanese American soldiers were assigned to a single segregated fighting unit, which became one of the most highly decorated units in the history of the U.S. Army. Sixth, as young Japanese American men turned eighteen, many were anxious to join the army and enter the ranks of what some regarded as America's best fighting unit. These new recruits were prepared to run any risk for their country, the United States. It is with this definition of situation that Shibutani's story starts.

By mid-1944, people in the United States could see an end to the war in Europe, perhaps in less than a year, but an end to the war in Asia seemed much further off. So by late 1944, the army stopped sending new Japanese American recruits to replenish its units in Europe, where they had been fighting Germans and Italians, and began sending them to language school at Fort Snelling in Minnesota. The troops sent to Fort Snelling for language training were supposed to become interpreters for an anticipated invasion force to land in Japan.

The army wanted the kind of eager young spit-and-polish recruits it had come to expect Japanese American soldiers to be, and that was exactly the mind-set of recruits who stepped off the bus at the beginning of training. Then the symbolic interaction started. The few white officers assigned to this particular Japanese American group were regarded by many of the soldiers as insensitive racists who viewed the recruits as inferior because of their ancestry. Progressively, the recruits' definition of situation changed, as they had individual experiences with those few officers and, importantly, as they talked among themselves. Peer groups shaped an emerging collective awareness. Within peer groups, as recruits shared their experiences with one another and talked about them to the point of shaping a collective interpretation of events and definition of situation, they decided that "the Army" was "chicken shit," a place where people felt they spent their time doing a lot of meaningless things, without effective coordination and often without apparent forethought. Quite naturally, their views and feelings were aimed at the whole army, even though their experience was quite localized to a few people and a relatively small number of events and encounters. This is a generalizable observation that can be communicated in the form of an axiom.

Social Location Axiom: *People tend to think that what they have personally encountered or heard from the people closest to them is authentic and representative and generally true of the way the world is.*

When definitions of situation changed, the nature of role behavior was quick to follow. Some soldiers assumed roles as "ring leaders" and actively organized efforts to subvert training activity. In the Fort Snelling case, the situation deteriorated to the point that the recruits began trying to be "screw up" soldiers in order to make their officers look bad. (To the American military's credit, it learned from the Fort Snelling case. It should also be mentioned that the military was one of the first parts of U.S. society to racially integrate, in the late 1940s. The U.S. military really led America's racial integration and has played a key role in socializing people to judge others on the basis of responsible performance rather than skin color.)

Shibutani was an intellectual grandchild of George Herbert Mead. That is to say, Shibutani's friend and teacher was the young student who took over Mead's role at the University of Chicago. That was one-time Chicago Bear's football player Herbert Blumer. As Blumer's own work matured, and with his 1969 book, *Symbolic Interactionism,* he became the most articulate spokesperson for the view that "society is symbolic interaction."[4] But while Blumer articulated the intellectual position, it was work such as Shibutani's that proved the point with extraordinarily detailed observation. The group of soldiers Shibutani studied seemed almost predestined to be model recruits instead of "mess ups." The army's structure, plus family needs and anticipatory socialization, almost guaranteed that this group would be exemplary spit-and-polish soldiers. So what happened? The company of recruits took on a life of its own as soon as people began to interact. Orientation to the wider setting (in this case, the army) was redefined in light of direct experience and emerging relationships within the unit. Shibutani was particularly struck by the importance of peer groups, or groups of equals we associate with, and reference groups, or the groups we look to as yardsticks for measuring our own performance. A lot of socialization, or learning about behavior and expectations, takes place in these groups, as does anticipatory socialization, or learning about behavioral expectations applying to some role we expect to enter in the future. These are ideas found throughout the symbolic interactionist literature, and they provide us with predictive insight about socialization.

Principle of Socialization: *Other things being equal, socialization is likely to be most effective to the degree that the person being socialized (a) depends on the socializing agent, (b) trusts the socializing agent, and*

(c) has an opportunity to act out or practice new norms and roles with peers.

One more example may serve to further illustrate the extent to which society really is symbolic interaction. The United States has gone from a society in which women were relegated to subservient positions in all walks of life to something closer to parity in many job sectors, and all in a single generation. A massive social transformation like this requires new laws, changes in school policy, and so forth. But as much anything else, symbolic interactionists feel that it takes one-on-one communication to open minds and change worldviews. Symbolic interactionists maintain that expanding horizons is something that sometimes has to be done the hard way, one person at a time, through challenging interpersonal encounters rife with symbolic meaning. Interactionists are inclined to feel that everything starts with discussion and symbolic encounter. They tend to believe that laws are only passed, and changes in occupational structure only emerge, after receptive ground is tediously prepared. To the extent that they are right, society really is symbolic interaction, and people really do have agency.

THE IOWA SCHOOL OF SYMBOLIC INTERACTION

The first long-running debate among symbolic interactionists concerned the source of fluidity in social encounters. Does interaction among people in a setting produce change purely out of happenstance? For example, consider an instance in which Aaron turns on the garbage disposal just as Joe is talking, resulting in Sally mishearing Joe and inaccurately concluding he is making a snide comment, to which Sally responds with anger and Joe counters with distain, which makes Sally counter/counter with disgust and Joe counter/counter/counter by storming out, leaving Sally feeling contempt and Joe looking for new friends, or a game of pickup basketball. If only Aaron had not turned on the garbage disposal at that very moment, Sally and Joe might have remained friends for life. This is the kind of scenario Chicago school interactionists are alert to. Society is symbolic interaction. Things change because people change them through their actions and reactions; change sometimes grows out of planned events and sometimes is rooted in unplanned or coincidental events. But how people act and react in making this change is highly fluid as far as Chicago interactionists are concerned.

Symbolic interactionists of the Chicago school see this kind of unfolding occur in real life, and they look for it. But there is a way to be a symbolic interactionist without giving so much credence to happenstance. That is, it is possible to think that society is symbolic interaction, with roles and relationships given their real shape and texture by the people immediately embroiled in the situation, and still nevertheless view outcomes as predictable. This describes the view of symbolic interactionists of the Iowa school and their intellectual descendants. They believe events tend toward predictable outcomes as a result of having a particular combination of personalities come together.

Imagine a strong-willed adult who yearns to be in charge, yet who must always take orders at work. This person also happens to hunger for much more "stuff" than the household budget can afford. Furthermore, this individual is married to a humble, unassuming person who doesn't make much money at work but tries to be content with what life gives. Now for a question: Is this marriage likely to be a carbon copy of every other marriage? Iowa school symbolic interactionists would say "no," because the "core self-concepts" of these people will persistently push interaction in a consistent direction.

Similar dynamics have been observed in organizations. Bosses who have doubts about their own ability commonly react in a predictable way. When confronting situations, they generally tend to retreat to role scripts. We see a very different pattern of reaction among those who are self-confident. They tend to respond to situations by moving away from routine and showing more tolerance of ambiguity. People in positions of authority with little self-assurance often tend to redefine roles in the direction of more routine, greater ritual in interpersonal relationships, and more power games. By way of contrast, people in positions of authority with high self-assurance often tend to redefine roles in the direction of less routine, less ritual in interpersonal relationships, and fewer power games.[5]

This issue presents a nice contrast of how different groups of theorists would approach the situation. All interactionists would be interested in distinctions that arise within the particular relationship and would be studying how these distinctions develop. Symbolic interactionists of the Iowa school emphasized that core self-concepts of the people in a relationship will persistently push interaction in a consistent, predictable direction. Long-run outcomes are constrained by a mix of personalities.

However, symbolic interactionists of the Chicago school countered that each ongoing relationship can easily become more distinctive and individualized over time as the course of events unfolds. Personality (core self) is thought to exert less influence. Eventual outcomes are thought to be more fluid and less predictable. But symbolic interactionists of all kinds credit people with having agency, and therefore being able to reshape the world they inhabit. This is to some degree different from conflict theorists who focus on the consistent pressures placed on people by their location in the class structure. From the perspective of conflict theory, long-run outcomes receive their basic contour from systems of wealth and privilege. And structural–functionalists focus on the consistent pressures placed on people by existing cultural patterns, institutional arrangements, and legal restraints. Structural–functionalists believe long-run outcomes are constrained by a variety of pressures originating in all those institutional spheres of activity.

The Chicago versus Iowa debate raises a serious issue. What determines the unique configuration that each marriage gravitates toward over time? People informed by the Iowa school are inclined to think core self-concept is continually injected into interaction, and often in critical ways, at turning-point moments. But people informed by the Chicago school are more likely to withhold a prediction about final outcomes because they are conscious that events can take unexpected twists and turns, and because they tend to think core self ultimately takes a backseat to the "situational self." If the core self is switched off a lot of the time, which is a premise built into Mead's Chicago school description of interaction in *Mind, Self, and Society,* then outcomes of any single interaction will be harder to predict, because the baggage of core self will not always be contaminating every encounter and dictating the contour of every outcome.[6] If "core self" is switched off, or at least turned down most of the time, each single situation presents a new set of possible choices. The range of outcomes increases geometrically with all the permutations and combinations involved in long chains of interaction. But Iowa school interactionists do not believe the core self is switched off or turned down that easily. They think core self actually gets amplified precisely at those emotion-laden moments when a person has to consider an adjustment that could make a difference.

It was Manford Kuhn who led sociologists at the University of Iowa to explore the role of core self-concept in determining people's reactions to situations. Part of the method he and his colleagues pioneered was to ask people to answer the simple question "Who am I?" by writing down words or phrases to describe themselves.[7] It turns out that many people tend to define who they are in terms of key roles they occupy. "I am mother/father, daughter/son, sister/brother, student, employee, boy-friend/girlfriend, sport player, team member." These are all nouns, and they suggest a strong identification with the social structural positions people occupy. Other people respond with adjectives that have more to do with style or quality of performance in roles than with precise social structural position. "I am smart, hardworking, clever, diligent," and so forth. It is hard to deny that on some level, sense of core self is a kind of baggage we carry with us from place to place. We all carry baggage, but seldom stop to calculate how that baggage may influence our perceptions and alter our subsequent behavior. This is what Manford Kuhn and his colleagues of the Iowa school of interaction call on us to do. The Iowa/Chicago debate will ultimately be resolved, when we articulate theoretical principles explaining when and how core self shuts off to allow itself to be superceded by situational factors.

To summarize, a long-running debate focused on the degree to which change in an interaction setting is (a) fluid and relatively unpredictable, because the activated self-concept tends to be "situational" and therefore highly variable from moment to moment, or (b) relatively predictable, be-cause the stable core-self aspects of personality people bring into a situa-tion push the flow of events in a more or less consistent and predictable direction. There has been plenty of interesting work done by sociologists attracted to this question. We have found, for example, that people who feel they are being evaluated in unjustifiably positive terms sometimes act in ways that convey the fact that they actually do not deserve such a high rating. In other words, some people subconsciously seem to shape inter-actions to make the way they look to others correspond with what they believe themselves to be really like. This was a position advanced by David Heise in what he described as affect control theory in his 1979 book, *Understanding Events*, which looks deep down inside people where the core self lives.[8]

One of the difficulties in dealing with this subject is conceptual impreci-sion leading people to use terms in different ways without fully appreci-ating the differences of meaning that are masked by sloppy use of lan-guage. To illustrate, "self" is often confused with "identity." But how we see ourselves in terms of qualities, which are the real substance of who we are as individuals (i.e., the core self), is not the same as our identity.

Having an "identity" is feeling that our memberships in groups or social categories are very important, making those memberships salient in our decision making. This normally happens when we realize people relate to us in terms of our group memberships rather than because of the quality of our individual performance or the content of our individual character. For instance, many of the people who have a strong sense of racial/ethnic identity are the people who have learned (from experience) to expect that they will be treated differently by appreciable numbers of people because of their race/ethnicity and not because of anything they have done or said or are individually responsible for.

There is a good reason sociological theorists let one another define concepts however they want to. This kind of tolerance for individuality of approach allows people to have latitude to carry their thinking out to its conclusion. But that means readers need to be alert to the definitions different writers use. Take the time to think conceptually in order to avoid misunderstanding the author's points. It is important for sociologists to strive as much as possible for conceptual precision in order to communicate accurately and avoid having our ideas misinterpreted.

DRAMATURGY

Symbolic interactionism of both the Chicago and Iowa varieties explores the work of *coconstruction* as people modify their relationships over time with the natural unfolding of interaction. Nothing stays the same. Not only can new feelings be created, but old feelings atrophy if they are not revitalized. We are all familiar with the example of young married people, very much in love, turning into couch potatoes with seemingly independent relationships with the same living-room television screen. Unless people in love do things to keep the fire alive, that love atrophies. Maintaining feelings takes work (the second law of thermodynamics). And if married people are fortunate enough to keep the fire alive, being passionately and playfully in love at fifty or sixty or seventy means something different from being passionately and playfully in love at twenty or thirty or forty. That certain "something" does not happen automatically. It needs to be molded and shaped and fabricated or it does not happen. And when it does happen, it does not stay around unless actively and continually enticed to stay. Note, then, that the defining feature of the symbolic interactionist perspective is concern with people mutually interacting in ways that shape change in the relationships. For both the Chicago and Iowa interactionists, this is collaborative work. When Blumer said "society is symbolic interaction," he could (as a former football player) have just as correctly said "symbolic interaction is a team sport." This is very important to remember when coming to really understand symbolic interactionism. The shape of change evolves within the give and take of interaction, within the relationship, among the people embroiled in relationships.

Dramaturgy is different, even though most people think of it as a variety of symbolic interactionism because it has many surface similarities with the Chicago and Iowa schools. Specifically, dramaturgical analysis focuses on the way people symbolically communicate in order to project views or convey impressions. Dramaturgical analysis, nicely summarized in Erving Goffman's 1959 book, *The Presentation of Self in Everyday Life,* specifically deals with impression management. Goffman presumes "all the world as a stage" and uses the theatrical concepts of a "front stage" (what the audience sees), a world of controlled and manipulated impressions broadcast outward for the consumption of others, and a "back stage" (what the actors know), a world of more honest and sincere interaction that few people are privy to.[9]

We are all familiar with front stage efforts at "impression management." It makes itself apparent whenever anyone is straining to look impressive. "Look at me. I am very cool, and also smart, clever. . . ." Goffman's focus was on the crafted images, usually positive, that people try to project of themselves. And we can, of course, also speak of altercasting, whereby one person tries to portray someone else by projecting crafted, often negative, images of that person.[10] Altercasting may prove to be an important concept when symbolic interaction is integrated with structural–functionalism and conflict theory, because altercasting is a major way in which feedback is distorted and conflict plays itself out.

Impression management and altercasting are quite common, although certainly more common in some environments than others. The very fact everyone understands what "impression management" means is proof enough that Goffman identified something that is very real. But while most symbolic interactionists feel comfortable identifying dramaturgy as an interactionist perspective, there is a fundamental distinction between Chicago and Iowa on one hand and dramaturgy on the other. The Chicago and Iowa frameworks are both about coconstructed change, which has genuine if not always pleasant character. Impression management is about a relatively static and fictional image that is projected from a single source and aimed at a receiver. The focus is not on what is cocrafted by two people synergistically changing what they have. It is on one person's projection of an illusion he hopes other people will respond to as real. Recognizing this distinction makes it easier to appreciate the real root concerns of the symbolic interactionist traditions. By contrasting Iowa and Chicago with dramaturgy, we can more fully appreciate that symbolic interactionists of the Iowa school and, even more, the Chicago school are like remodelers in the construction industry. They focus on how people can work together to modify what they started with, transforming it into something else. This recognition ultimately sets the stage for an integration of symbolic interactionism with the structural–functionalist and conflict perspectives.

ROLE THEORY

From the beginning, some symbolic interactionists were grappling with the challenge of dealing with social structural realities. The fact that there are people in recognizable "student" roles all over the world, doing very similar things with other people who are in recognizable "teacher" roles, often interacting in similar places recognizable as "schools," is enough to suggest that we individuals do not simply go out and imaginatively construct completely unique worlds for ourselves. Instead, we inherit some things by virtue of being born in a particular society. What we inherit includes a preexisting framework of social institutions (which structural–functionalists are especially interested in) and a preexisting framework of class and stratification (which conflict theorists are particularly interested in). We take those preexisting things that we inherit and then shape them somewhat as we take one small corner of the social world and make it our own (which the symbolic interactionists are particularly interested in). And this always involves negotiated exchanges of different kinds (which the exchange theorists are particularly interested in). All this is captured in the Principle of Role Redefinition, developed in chapter 9.

We are not completely "free" agents when shaping our own little corner of the world, because other people are also in the mix and seeking their own accommodations. We have agency along with others, and it is together that we shape and mold the reality we will live with. This idea is nicely conveyed by Peter Berger and Thomas Luchmann in their 1967 book, *The Social Construction of Reality*.[11] We are all social carpenters and psychological plumbers and management electricians engaged in constantly remodeling that portion of the social world we traverse. But the remodeling jobs each of us engage in normally take place within or are attached to some preexisting framework defined by the institutions and organizations and class structure that permeate the society. We make our entry into and connection with those institutions and organizations and class structure through the roles we occupy.

Role theorists try to deal with structural realities while keeping faith with the most basic tenets of symbolic interactionism. They do so by focusing on roles (rights and obligations defining what would be expected of anyone occupying a particular position) and on relationships (aspects of role performance that are unique to particular combinations of people and would most likely change in the event that the role occupants are replaced).[12] Of course, all sociologists recognize that roles are among the basic building blocks of social organization. They are the tether posts around which people orchestrate and shape their lives.

Role theorists ask fundamental questions about roles and relationships inside of institutions and organizations. How is it that people get assigned the roles they have? Why do those roles have the general form that they do? Once people are in a role relationship, how likely are they to individualize that relationship, and how does that process of improvisational change really occur? What role does the wider environment play in allowing people to "make their own deal" or in pressuring people to "pull their own weight." These are the basic questions role theorists pose, in the work of people like Ralph Turner in his 1990 article on role change.[13]

William Goode was one of many important developers of role theory. Goode's concept of "role strain," or the demand overload we experience when we consider all of our various role commitments and obligations, is one of the most powerful concepts sociologists have.[14] How do people respond as role strain mounts? Arlie Hochschild explores the challenges posed by role strain in her 1997 study of the difficulty of balancing work and family. She argues that role strain is a pivotal factor driving social change in contemporary America. Hochschild's research demonstrates that as people spend more time at work, family members have less time and emotional energy to give each other. The very texture of our lives is changing as a result. People used to be relatively private at work and look to the family for the bulk of their socioemotional support. But increasingly, large numbers of people find that they are growing more private in the family context while looking to the workplace for the bulk of their socioemotional support.[15]

This makes role theory a natural bridge between symbolic interactionism and structural–functionalism, as illustrated by Hage and Powers in *Post-Industrial Lives*. Complex organizations, social institutions, and class structure are all real, and they do determine a great deal. But life in them absolutely necessitates a degree of adjustment. The types and degree of adjustment required are variable and open to social science explanation. But adjustment is required and that adjustment occurs through a process of symbolic interaction.

While the old-style bureaucratic workplace called for comparatively little adjustment beyond accommodation to rules, the innovation-producing workplace emblematic of the postindustrial economy requires more interactive play and flexibility from workers. Increasingly, the individual who has the best idea at the moment, not the person with the highest semipermanent job title, is the one people listen to. More people have a career trajectory of being shifted from one project team to another every several months or couple of years, instead of going to work in the same section of the same building with the same people for one, two, three, or four decades. And to the degree that the teams are engaged in developing or delivering innovative or customized products and services, there needs to be a lot more nuanced communication among team members and clients and outside venders, to get as precisely as possible at a good solution for the problem at hand.

All this implies something about structural–functionalist thinking and the relationship between symbolic interactionism and structural–functionalism. We should not ask whether early structural–functionalists were right when they took structural determinacy for granted. Nor should we ask if the early symbolic interactionists were right when they took human agency for granted. A more contemporary structural–functionalist view would be that, to be able to function, organizations need people to exercise agency. Symbolic interaction, then, is an absolutely necessary process that has to unfold within organizations in order for those organizations to be able to function. But organizations that need to generate a steady stream of innovations have to encourage more agency than organizations doing the same routine work over and over again. Symbolic interactionists have always appreciated that there are practical limits to agency in any environment. A structural–functional approach to this subject gives us a way of understanding the variations in those limits, at least in complex organizations, based on the goals of those organizations and their organizational structure. This affirms one of the starting points of this book. The different theoretical perspectives do not invalidate each other. Instead, they work together in an additive way. Each gives us a different piece of a bigger puzzle.

To say that symbolic interaction is a functional requisite for organizations does not end social science inquiry. From a science point of view, it only gets our inquiry off to a good start by identifying types of variability we need to explain. Organizations are not all the same in terms of the amount of agency they need people to exercise, or the issues over which agency needs to be exercised for the organization to function effectively. Those are things we want to understand and explain. But we already have a first approximation answer in the form of the Innovation/Complexity Principle, introduced in chapter 6. The same conditions that privilege certain alliance structures over hierarchy and markets also necessitate the exercise of more agency in order for inter- and intraorganizational activity to be coordinated effectively. More agency is necessary where complexity and other conditions require innovation. The functional requirements of that sort of organization are best satisfied in an environment rich in symbolic interaction.[16]

RECAP

Symbolic interaction is distinctive in its focus, not just on individual agency, but on co-agency. Symbolic interactionists focus on ways in which meaning is cooperatively constructed. Everyone has some voice, and arrangements that are concluded are a synthesis resulting from give and take. The outcomes of that give and take are influenced by the self-concepts and identities people bring with them into new situations. But the degree to which self-concepts and identities affect outcomes is still under study. Class structure, institutional arrangements, and location in organizations greatly influence people's lives, but wherever people find themselves they still use their social skills to modify and temper their social surroundings, often by modifying the roles in which they find themselves. Keeping this in mind helps us connect symbolic interaction with the conflict and structural–functionalist perspectives.

NOTES

1. George Herbert Mead, *Mind, Self, and Society* (Chicago: University of Chicago Press, 1934).

2. Jerald Hage and Charles Powers, *Post-Industrial Lives* (Thousand Oaks, Calif.: Sage, 1992).

3. Tamotsu Shibutani, *The Derelicts of Company K* (Berkeley: University of California Press, 1978).

4. Herbert Blumer, *Symbolic Interactionism* (Englewood Cliffs, N.J.: Prentice-Hall, 1969).

5. Hage and Powers, *Post-Industrial Lives*, 132.

6. George Herbert Mead, *Mind, Self, and Society* (Chicago: University of Chicago Press, 1934).

7. Manford Kuhn and Thomas McPhartland, "An Empirical Investigation of Self Attitudes," *American Sociological Review* 19, no. 1 (February 1954): 68–76.

8. David Heise, *Understanding Events* (New York: Cambridge University Press, 1979).

9. Erving Goffman, *The Presentation of Self in Everyday Life* (New York: Doubleday, 1959).

10. Eugene Weinstein and Paul Deutschberger, "Some Dimensions of Altercasting," *Sociometry* 26 (1963): 454–66.

11. Peter Berger and Thomas Luchmann, *The Social Construction of Reality* (New York: Doubleday, 1967).

12. Louis Zurcher, *Social Roles* (Beverly Hills, Calif.: Sage, 1983).

13. Ralph Turner, "Role Change," *Annual Review of Sociology* 16 (1990): 87–110.

14. William Goode, "A Theory of Role Strain," *American Sociological Review* 25 (1960): 483–96.

15. Arlie Hochschild, *Time Bind: When Work Becomes Home and Home Becomes Work* (New York: Holt, 1997).

16. Hage and Powers, *Post-Industrial Lives*, 211–15.

SOME TERMS TO KNOW

Peer Group. A group of equals we associate closely with.

Reference Group. A group we look to as a yardstick for measuring our own performances.

Socialization. Learning from others, especially about behavioral expectations.

Anticipatory Socialization. A type of socialization, specifically, learning about behavioral expectations applying to some role we expect to enter in the future.

Core Self-Concept. Traits we see as deeply ingrained in and significantly defining our character.

Situational Self-Concept. A sense of how our performance is in a particular and immediate situation.

Role Strain. The cumulative weight of all the demands a person confronts in his or her various roles.

Altercasting. Setting someone up to be viewed in a particular way by others.

AXIOM AND PRINCIPLE REVIEW

Social Location Axiom: *People tend to think that what they have personally encountered or heard from the people closest to them is authentic and representative and generally true of the way the world is.*

Principle of Socialization: *Other things being equal, socialization is likely to be most effective to the degree that the person being socialized (a) depends on the socializing agent, (b) trusts the socializing agent, and (c) has an opportunity to act out or practice new norms and roles with peers.*

CHAPTER REVIEW TEST

Check your answers against the key at the back of the book. If you get any wrong, reread chapter 13, thinking about it as you go, before moving on to chapter 14.

1. What is the most fundamental difference between dramaturgical analysis and mainstream (Chicago or Iowa) symbolic interactionism?

2. Symbolic interactionists of the Iowa school believe that outcomes in social situations are rather predictable. What makes outcomes relatively predictable, in their view?

3. Define:
   a. Identity
   b. Role

APPLICATION EXERCISE

Think about a turning point event in a relationship you or someone you know was in or is now in. What was the relationship like before the turning point event? What happened? What was the relationship like after the turning point event? How much, if at all, do you think that core self-concepts drove the perceptions and influenced the actions of people in this situation? How much, if at all, did new understandings unfold as a kind of synthesis genuinely influenced by input of more than one person, in contrast with new meaning being the imposed will of one person, irrespective of the ideas and wishes of others?

14

EXCHANGE THEORY IN THE BACKGROUND

Everyone Has Motives

Exchange theory was rather slow to take shape as a self-identified perspective distinct from the other theoretical paradigms. Exchange was initially thought of as a generic concern of equal interest to everyone, with a few of the theorists working within the confines of each of the other perspectives taking special interest in exchange phenomena. But over time, those interested in exchange began talking more and more to one another and formulating strategies for trying to understand this aspect of social reality. As they did that, a perspective began to emerge that is somewhat distinct and deserves separate recognition and review.

THINKING OF EXCHANGE IN BROAD TERMS

When most Americans use the word "exchange," a financial sale or purchase is often the first thing that comes to mind. Would you rather buy a soda for $1 or a coffee for $2, or would you perhaps rather have free water from a drinking fountain and save your money? Would you rather spend a lot of money on a great sound system and eat peanut butter for a year or eat what you want and listen to the radio, or would you perhaps rather put your money in the bank or invest it in the stock market? Would you rather use the full-service pump at a gas station and pay more but get more service, or would you rather pay less, use the self-service pump, and just take the gas? In a sense, these are all utilitarian economic questions.

They suggest at least the possibility of rational calculation by weighing costs and benefits, with the determination of benefits influenced by some combination of personal taste and immediate need.

From the start, those sociologists who were most informed by utilitarian economics had a special interest in this kind of exchange. But what about other sociologists? It is important to stop and think about the fact that there is much more to "exchange" than commercial transactions. The early sociologists interested in exchange recognized that fact. When you say hello to someone and anticipate an acknowledgment in return, there is a kind of exchange going on. Think about how you feel when you say hello to someone, but that person fails to acknowledge you. Do you say hello the next time you see that person? That may depend on whether, deep down, you really consider this an exchange. If you offered your positive recognition as a "gift" in the truest sense of the term, freely given without regard to how it would be received or used, lack of acknowledgment does not matter. But if you offered your positive recognition to the other person in the expectation of receiving a certain amount of positive recognition back, then you may think twice about acknowledging the person next time.

Thought of as an exchange, recognizing others and not being recognized in return may be a bad trade, at least in the short-run. You lost face. In a way, your social capital experienced some deflation. And for what? For nothing, because your investment failed to yield the expected return, which was the pleasure of social acceptance, plus the upward value in your social capital that is implicit when others indicate (especially in public) that you are a person who is worth acknowledging. All this is as an exchange theorist might view it. Exchange theorists' axiomatic assumptions lead them to believe that people are often motivated by this kind of calculation.

The more you think conceptually about exchange, the more interesting it becomes. When you give a friend a birthday card and get some good feeling from seeing his or her surprise, is it an exchange? Or should it be considered an act of exchange only after the person does something for you in an act of reciprocity? How far does the "norm of reciprocity" extend in our society?[1] A norm of reciprocity does imply a kind of long-term exchange relationship, or at the very least that exchange is a mechanism people use to sustain their relationships.

Can it be thought of as an exchange when you give directions to a stranger in anticipation that someone else will return the favor to you the next time you find yourself a stranger in a strange place? Indeed, many people conceive of every back-and-forth transmission as exchange. Part of the challenge of exchange theory, and a reason exchange theorists enjoy interacting with each other so much, is the fun in talking about what really does or does not constitute an exchange. One thing exchange theorists tend to agree on is that the individual act of a single exchange is a rudimentary and fundamental building block of all social organization.

SYMBOLIC EXCHANGE

From the start, both Mead and Durkheim conceived of human interaction in terms of symbolic exchange. For Mead, interaction is based on exchange of gestures that are packed with meaning. He even wrote about symbolic interaction as an exchange of gestures. And for Durkheim, awareness of the exchange dimension of interaction bordered on mystical. Do you recall Durkheim's preoccupation, really almost an obsession, with integration? And what integrates modern industrial society more than anything else? According to Durkheim, the answer is division of labor grounded in complex networks of economic exchanges people have to rely on to acquire all the goods and services they cannot provide for themselves. And how many of sociology's other founding figures were economists who initially focused on exchange aspects of social life and then broadened out? We can start with Marx, Weber, Pareto, and Veblen. But Durkheim believed that exchange integrated the society in ways that went beyond provision of goods and services in a differentiated society. He was most intrigued by symbolic aspects of exchange. He viewed exchange as a way validating the significance of relationships, by heralding the importance of those relationships.

Durkheim's attention was always riveted to symbolic exchange. The most important ritual behaviors have, as their primary purpose (in other words, as their main function), to acknowledge and celebrate the connections linking people with one another. This view receives its clearest expression in Durkheim's last great work, *Elementary Forms of Religious Life*, published in 1912.[2] It was through reading *Elementary Forms of Religious Life* that the British and French anthropological communities became aware of Durkheim's functional theorizing and began to apply his ideas. Durkheim's *Elementary Forms* and the anthropological works that followed, written by people such as Siegfried Nadel (who profoundly influenced role theory, exchange theory, and network theory in sociology with his short conceptual book *The Theory of Social Structure*),[3] focused explicitly on rituals affirming membership and celebrating the distinctiveness of groups. Of all the rituals studied by the early structural–functionalists, exchange rituals gained the most attention because they gave clues about alliances and affiliations that had hitherto gone unobserved or had been underappreciated.

The first of the anthropological works to follow Durkheim's conceptual lead was Bronislaw Malinowski's 1922 study of the Trobriand Islands, *Argonauts of the Western Pacific*.[4] A key facet of Malinowski's study was his report on a decidedly noneconomic exchange of armlets and necklaces known as the "kula ring." The Trobriand Islands consist of a circular archipelago. In a kula ring, there is an exchange of armlets moving in one direction within the circular island chain, and of necklaces moving in the other direction. The armlets and necklaces are made of local materials, so the exchange is of limited material value on the surface of it. This is not a barter of something one has excess of for something one would like to have more of. Instead, kula exchange is understood as an opportunity to revive and reaffirm a prior relationship (whether it be a relationship of equals or a subordinate/superordinate relationship). It may interest readers to know that some of the implications of this exchange were worked out in a book (*The Gift*, 1925) written by one of the lone members of Durkheim's cadre of young protégés to survive World War I, Durkheim's own nephew, Marcel Mauss.[5] Mauss helped carry Durkheim's theoretical orientation (influencing overlapping but distinct structural–functionalist and exchange perspectives) into anthropology, where it was later recaptured by Robert K. Merton and others for reexport back to sociology. It is also worth noting that this exchange orientation validates the symbolic interactionist view that relationships must be actively reinvigorated in order to be sustained. A relationship that is not actively sustained on a symbolic level will be muted and will atrophy.

Symbolic Exchange Axiom: *Nonutilitarian signs of recognition and acceptance are the principal ways through which social ties are revived and affirmed.*

Exchange theorists, over and over again in setting after setting, have discovered that exchange rituals are a common instrument people use for symbolically affirming relationships and keeping them alive. Sociological treatments of symbolic exchange focus on gift giving as a strategy for cementing friendships and affirming alliances in everyday life. A perfect illustration is found in Christmas and Hanukkah gift-giving practices. In the 1920s, when the research for *Middletown* was conducted, Americans were giving many more gifts to neighbors than they do now. Perhaps Americans were more generous eighty years ago. But exchange theorists offer another explanation for the change in gift-giving practices. The prevailing pattern was to give simple, inexpensive, homemade gifts such as Christmas cookies. Such gifts have mainly symbolic value, specifically announcing "I have the time for you and you are one of the people I might reasonably call on to make time for me if I ever need help." In *Middletown*, gift recipients typically included people living up and down the road who might do things such as give you a ride to work if you, for example, had a flat tire; they also included a broad swath of extended family living anywhere nearby. That was, after all, the 1920s, when car batteries were less reliable, when car tires frequently went flat, and when bosses were far more insistent that people started the workday precisely on time. It was also an age when people put in the electrical wiring in their homes themselves, fixed their own roof leaks, and even built their own garages and barns on weekends (in "barn raisings") with the help of family, friends, and neighbors. Exchange theorists do not think Americans gave more gifts in the 1920s because they were more generous then. Exchange theorists think Americans gave more gifts because their pattern of life was different. They had more periodic dependence on others and consequently needed to symbolically affirm more relationships.[6]

RATIONAL CHOICE AND GAME THEORY

Most versions of exchange theory rely on a rational choice model of behavior. Exchange decisions are often made on the basis of simple cost/benefit calculations such as those described by Homans in *Social Behavior, Its Elementary Forms*.[7] Rational choice theorists have made steady strides in trying to develop and test their explanations. One of the interesting applications, illustrating the versatility of rational choice analysis, is the discovery that there seems to be a balance between what religious congregations demand from parishioners and what they offer to parishioners. This idea was first suggested by Peter Berger in his book *The Sacred Canopy*, and it was more systematically developed in a 1994 paper by Larry Iannaccone.[8] Some congregations ask a great deal (mandatory tithing, for example) and offer a great deal (for instance, help finding jobs for congregation members who are unemployed). Other congregations ask comparatively little and in return offer comparatively little by way of tangible benefits (aside from the aspect of guidance in getting to heaven). Congregations that ask little but give a great deal of material support go bankrupt, and those that ask a great deal and give little in return tend not to survive because (Iannaccone hypothesizes) people find a better deal elsewhere.

As aptly pointed out by Homans, drawing from both utilitarian economics and behavioral psychology, rational choice is essentially a calculation of expected costs and probable benefits of possible courses of action relative to possible alternative courses of action.[9] By doing what we are doing right now, we are accepting expected costs in the anticipation of benefits we deem probable. We are simultaneously forgoing the benefits we think we could get by doing something else. In other words, there are opportunity costs. Even when we are continuing in an old pattern of action, there are still rational calculations to be made. The last bite we took may have satisfied our hunger (satiation, in psychological terms), so food may lose its appeal for a few hours (the law of diminishing returns, in economic terms). This presents people at a restaurant with the classical situation for rationally calculating the point of marginal utility. You and a date stop at a restaurant on the way home from a movie because you are hungry and want a slice of pie. The pie is good, and the cost is little enough that you are glad you stopped at the restaurant. You conclude that you made an accurate rational choice decision because it seems to you that satisfying your hunger was worth the money you spent. Then the waiter comes and asks you if you would like another slice of pie (at the same price, because the menu hasn't changed). But the first slice of pie satiates your appetite sufficiently so that you are no longer very hungry. Does the small bit of hunger that remains make it worthwhile buying another slice of pie, or have you reached the point of marginal utility at which keeping your money to spend on something else seems wiser?

The pie example is interesting, because it can be used to make Homan's concerns come to life. If hunger was the whole reason for stopping, why not go to the grocery store for a half gallon of milk, a package of celery, and a canister of peanut butter to take home? This would probably be cheaper than stopping at the restaurant for pie, and the peanut butter approach might have the added benefit of allowing for leftovers to be stored in preparation for the eventuality of hunger tomorrow. Or by going to the restaurant, were you actually doing more than satisfying hunger? Might it be that you were also "buying time" to talk with your date without the prying eyes of family members or roommates around? Just what is it that makes this restaurant stop worth the cost? And whoever made up the rule that a movie followed by a stop at a restaurant makes for a good date? Why not go on a date to the coin-operated laundry with dirty clothes and talk while the clothes are being washed and dried? That would be very practical, making the Laundromat the economically rational place to go. But, as Homans pointed out, why people want what they want is sociological rather than economic. And how individuals project costs and weigh probabilities are as likely to be dominated by sociological factors as by economic calculations.

When rational calculation is assumed, outcomes can be predicted and the consequences of various changes in scenario can be worked out using game theory, as long as players are willing and able to make assumptions about the people whose behavior is being modeled. But the utility of game theory is strictly limited to situations in which the number of pertinent variables is limited and relationships among variables are reasonably well known, as explained by Harsanyi and Selten in their 1977 book, *A General Theory of Equilibrium in Games and Social Situations.*[10] For rational choice in general and game theory in particular, one of the most vexing issues is that of "externalized costs." Externalized costs are side effects the actor is allowed to ignore: unrepaired damage, depleted resources, and expenses absorbed by others. If the state provides roads and water for a factory that does not pay taxes, the cost of transport and utility infrastructure is paid by the society at large. That portion of the costs of production is socialized.

Fixed costs are also important to calculate. When a fishing company borrows money to purchase a large fishing trawler, the loan has to be repaid, with interest, whether the ship sails or not. If the ship sails, the crew needs to be paid whether the ship puts out all its nets or only half its nets. The costs of operation are largely fixed. So to improve cost-benefit ratios, the ship owners need to stay at sea as long as possible, keep as many miles of net out as possible, and catch as many fish as possible. The more financially overextended a business is, the closer it is to losing collateral if it does not maximize its "revenue stream," and therefore, the more incentive it has for externalizing costs. When indigenous men fishing in small boats use explosives to "fish" but in so doing destroy coral reefs and reduce their future catch for a larger and easier catch today, you know costs are being externalized. And when factory trawlers deplete fish stocks by laying out miles of net, you know costs are being externalized.

BALANCING POWER IN EXCHANGE

Richard Emerson outlined a dramatically different approach to the study of exchange in a path-breaking 1962 paper, "Power-Dependency Relations."[11] Emerson started by describing simple exchange relations in terms of dependency and power. The more a person needs what she gets from an exchange, and the fewer alternatives she has for satisfying her needs elsewhere, then the more dependent the person is on continuation of the relationship and the more power that individual's exchange partners will have to extract compliance as a condition for continuing in the exchange relationship.

This seems straightforward enough. But Emerson developed these points and reached conclusions that were anything but obvious, and these have been elaborated on by other scholars over the years.[12] First, conceiving of exchange in terms of shifting patterns of power and dependence leads to the conclusion that all participants in exchange are to some degree dependent on continuation of the relationship, even if only in a tiny way, because (exchange theorists presume) every party gets something useful out of the exchange. It also suggests that any change in the terms of exchange rearranges patterns of dependence. So when a more powerful exchange partner forces a more dependent exchange partner to "pay" a higher price for continuation of the relationship, the more powerful exchange partner suddenly becomes somewhat more dependent than he had been, and consequently somewhat less powerful, at the same time that the person who started out more dependent and less powerful in the relationship now becomes more powerful (although perhaps somewhat poorer) than he had been. Hence, the relationship moves toward balance in power and dependence. For example, a really popular person in high school may not tolerate an unpopular student hanging around unless that less popular individual is obsequious and does things for Mr. or Ms. Popular. But if the less popular student feeds some craving the popular person has with obsequious behavior, then Mr. or Ms. Popular becomes more dependent on the less popular individual than the popular person had been previously. If that happens, the less popular individual might then demand something she wants, such as insider recognition, as an implicit condition of her continued participation in this exchange. A simplified illustration can be diagrammed to make sure the time progression that Emerson identified is clear (figure 14.1).

Figure 14.1 is, of course, a simple illustration. In this case, greater balance is brought to a relationship simply by changing the pricing structure. If costs go up for the person who started off as less powerful and go down for the person who started off as more powerful, then power and dependency move in the direction of balance.

What Emerson had the genius to recognize is illustrated in the case of my dentist. If my dentist raises fees and forces me to pay more to help subsidize his rather costly hobbies (such as hot-air ballooning) I become a more valued client. Then, exchange theorists might predict, my dentist is going to be more careful about my teeth because keeping me as a client helps keep his balloon in the air. I think I have a great dentist and I am grateful to be his client. I do not want anything to change. I pay promptly, and that is one of the things making me a good customer. When I have to work a dental appointment around my rather thick assortment of family and work obligations there is never a problem.

Were I to write a "me and my dentist" theory book, one of the conflict chapters might explore why I have better dental care now than when I was a child (my parents didn't have a lot of money, and medical attention was regarded as an option of last resort) or why my dental care right now (as a college professor with decent insurance and a salary substantially above the national average) is much better than the care received by anyone I know from a lower-income household. As a person informed by conflict theory, I see all kinds of problems with the way society distributes medical care. But even when I am wearing my hat as a conflict theorist, I

Figure 14.1. Balancing Power and Dependence by Redefining Terms of Exchange

	Person A		Person B	
	Power	*Dependence*	*Power*	*Dependence*
Time 1	more	less	less	more
Time 2	begins contributing less to the relationship		begins contributing more to the relationship	
Time 3	midlevel	midlevel	midlevel	midlevel

can still see an exchange analysis as valuable for what it illuminates. An important message of this book is that sociology's different theoretical frameworks are most useful when they are treated as mutually compatible rather than mutually exclusive.

Emerson predicates his exchange theory on the idea that power (the ability to extract compliance) is inversely related to dependence. If one party is more powerful in a relationship, that party can demand more, but in demanding more he becomes more dependent, and therefore is in less of a position to continue inflating costs.

Pivotal for Emerson is the notion that power imbalance will lead to some kind of change, with the result that the relationship will become more balanced over time, unless there are limits set on the demands exchange partners can place on each other. Such limits can be based on friendship ties, communal solidarity, custom, norm formation, administrative fiat, or law.

Power Imbalance Axiom: *Social settings tend to change in the direction of greater symmetry of power and dependence, or toward development of formal and informal limits on exploitation in nonsymmetric relationships.*

One obvious kind of change would be to have the more dependent person contribute more in the future than she did in the past, essentially paying more to sustain the relationship, or to have the more powerful person contribute less in the future while continuing to get just as much as she did in the past. Hypothetically, my dentist could raise his rates, or if I could not pay the higher rate, he might see me anyway but rush me through dental procedures more quickly, keeping me as a client but at less cost to himself. It is also quite possible that my dentist would continue to provide me with the same (exceptionally high quality) dental care, even if I could not pay. This points to the importance of data. If we have a lot of solid information about the things different dentists will or will not do pro bono, for whom, under what circumstances, and for what motives, we will be in a good position to add to, modify, or define limiting conditions for Emerson's ideas. Doing real science begins with theoretical ideas that can help us make predictions, and it then provides for an empirical test of those ideas with the idea of reflecting on and trying to correct, or add to or move beyond, the level of theoretical understanding we started with.

Emerson's real genius was to realize that there are social structural alterations beyond changes in individual pricing that can go a long way toward rectifying a power imbalance. Coalitions can form, as when farmers form a cooperative to sell their grain collectively. Greater division of labor can allow people to leave jobs characterized by labor oversupply and low wages, in favor of jobs characterized by labor undersupply and high wages. Other kinds of structural change can stabilize an imbalanced relationship by preventing the more powerful (less dependent) person from exploiting a power imbalance to his or her advantage. It often happens that norms can develop to limit the exploitation of a power imbalance. Hierarchical regulatory agencies and administrative controls within organizations can set boundaries preventing some forms of exploitation. That is why teachers cannot demand baby-sitting services or lawn mowing from their students. A teacher who offers extra credit in exchange for baby-sitting services might find that some students are interested, but few college administrators would regard this as a legitimate practice. Baby-sitting for money or even out of kindness, yes, but not for course credit.

The baby-sitting example is interesting because it introduces the concept of regulatory authority within an exchange theoretical rubric. We have also discussed regulatory control in our review of structural–functionalism and conflict theory. Drawing those ideas together, and especially within Emerson's framework, suggests a useful principle.

Principle of Regulation: *Other things being equal, the extension of regulatory control over new spheres of activity by a branch of government is a positive function of (a) the magnitude of externalized costs that are understood to result from unregulated activity, (b) the degree to which a regulatory vacuum compromises the government's claim that it protects people, and (c) the legitimacy of the regulatory extension, and it is a negative function of (d) the degree to which the government is already overburdened with other concerns and commitments.*

Why, one might ask, are we at this moment in time suddenly seeing much tighter regulation of smoking? A good theoretical principle tells us what the pertinent variables are if we want to explain differences between cases or change over time.

By thinking conceptually about simple exchange, Emerson was able to deduce conditions for the development of more complex social arrangements. He even put his ideas to the test in remote tribal areas of northern

Pakistan long before that region came under focus following September 11, 2001, applying exchange theory to the study of chieftain patterns. Of all the exchange perspectives developed, Emerson's scheme may ultimately offer the most promise. Even with Emerson, however, we are still left with Homans's most pressing questions unanswered: Why do people value what they value? How can we understand why the externalization of some costs are allowed, while the externalization of other costs are not allowed?

EXTENSIONS TO NETWORK THEORY

The exchange framework extends naturally to a body of literature sociologists refer to as network theory, which explores the nature of interconnections linking people. The way in which we are interconnected with others determines the range of choices open to us and the range of resources we have for exploiting opportunities. Mark Granovetter ignited excitement about network theory (already a part of the intellectual scene through the work of people like Nadel), defying conventional wisdom by offering a fresh new network explanation for the success of upper-middle-class people. In addition to all their other advantages, members of the upper middle class tend to maintain a comparatively wide range of comparatively shallow friendships. This network pattern tends to generate more job prospects than the network pattern that is more common among working-class people, a more narrow range of somewhat closer friendships. Close friendship networks tend to be small, homogeneous, closed, and therefore not very useful when people are trying to identify new and different potential opportunities. Whatever information or help one member of the circle can provide is likely to only replicate rather than add to whatever information and help every other member of the same social circle can provide. In contrast, someone with a heterogeneous range of shallow acquaintances is likely to hear of a wider assortment of opportunities. Each person in the network is likely to have information that adds to rather than merely replicating information available from others in the network.[13]

The link between network theory and exchange theory developed around norm formation. Normative rules tend to develop that constrain terms of exchange within networks.[14] These often take the form of understandings that limit the kinds of compliance more powerful parties extract from weaker parties. The will of people to subordinate themselves to rules is closely tied to the degree of dependence on the group and feelings of solidarity with the group.[15]

RECAP

Among sociology's four main explanatory perspectives, exchange theory was the last to take shape, and it is the one to be most formally systematized. The concept of dependence and the assumption that people act in ways designed to minimize dependence are central tenets of exchange theory. Exchange theorists have gone far beyond examination of individual exchange decisions to offer revealing insights about the emergence of system properties to limit and channel exchange. These include the appearance of coalitions, the formation of norms, the extension of regulatory controls, and changes in complexity of social networks. More than theorists of any other of sociology's main perspectives, exchange theorists have striven for a level of conceptual clarity that keeps them talking together (not past each other) with energy focused on explaining the appearance of the different kinds of social structural arrangements that are at the heart of sociology's subject matter.

NOTES

1. Alvin Gouldner, "The Norm of Reciprocity: A Preliminary Statement," *American Sociological Review* 25, no. 4 (April 1960): 161–77.

2. Emile Durkheim, *The Elementary Forms of Religious Life* (1912; reprint, New York: Free Press, 1954).

3. S. F. Nadel, *The Theory of Social Structure* (London: Cohen and West, 1956).

4. Bronislaw Malinowski, *Argonauts of the Western Pacific* (1922; reprint, New York: Dutton, 1950).

5. Marcel Mauss, *The Gift* (1925; reprint, New York: Norton, 1967).

6. Theodore Caplow, "Christmas Gifts and Kin Networks," *American Sociological Review* 47, no. 3 (June 1982): 383–92.

7. George Homans, *Social Behavior, Its Elementary Forms*, 2nd ed. (New York: Harcourt, Brace, Jovanovich, 1974).

8. Peter Berger, *The Sacred Canopy: Elements of a Sociological Theory of Religion*, 2nd ed. (New York: Random House, 1990); Larry Iannaccone, "Why Strict Churches Are Strong," *American Journal of Sociology* 99 (1994): 1006–1028.

9. Homans, *Social Behavior*.

10. John Harsanyi and Reinhard Selten, *A General Theory of Equilibrium in Games and Social Situations* (Cambridge: Cambridge University Press, 1977).

11. Richard Emerson, "Power–Dependency Relations," *American Sociological Review* 27, no. 1 (February 1962): 31–41.

12. Linda Molm and Karen Cook, "Social Exchange Networks," in *Sociological Perspectives on Social Psychology*, edited by K. Cook, G. Fine, and J. House (Boston: Allyn & Bacon, 1995).

13. Mark Granovetter, "The Strength of Weak Ties," *American Journal of Sociology* 78, no. 6 (May 1973): 1360–89.

14. See David Willer and Bo Anderson, eds., *Networks, Exchange, and Coercion* (New York: Elsevier, 1981).

15. Michael Hechter, *Principles of Group Solidarity* (Berkeley: University of California Press, 1987).

SOME TERMS TO KNOW

Externalized Costs. Side effects an actor is allowed to ignore: unrepaired damage, depleted resources, and expenses absorbed by others.

Dependence. The felt need to continue a relationship, which increases as desire for whatever the person gets out of the relationship increases and which diminishes with the availability of alternative sources of the same thing or suitable substitutes for it.

REVIEW OF AXIOMS AND PRINCIPLES

Symbolic Exchange Axiom: *Nonutilitarian signs of recognition and acceptance are the principal ways through which social ties are revived and affirmed.*

Power Imbalance Axiom: *Social settings tend to change in the direction of greater symmetry of power and dependence, or toward development of formal and informal limits on exploitation in nonsymmetric relationships.*

Principle of Regulation: *Other things being equal, the extension of regulatory control over new spheres of activity by a branch of government is a positive function of (a) the magnitude of externalized costs that are understood to result from unregulated activity, (b) the degree to which a regulatory vacuum compromises the government's claim that it protects people, and (c) the legitimacy of the regulatory extension, and it is a negative function of (d) the degree to which the government is already overburdened with other concerns and commitments.*

CHAPTER REVIEW TEST

Check your answers against the answer key in the back of the book. If you get any wrong, reread chapter 14, thinking about it as you go, before moving on to part IV of the book.

1. T F   Gift-giving patterns change as peoples' needs to rely on each other change.

2. T F   Changes in social structure can sometimes be explained in terms of efforts of people to escape unequal power in exchange relationships.

APPLICATION EXERCISE

Who, if anyone, have you given birthday cards to in the past twelve months? If you had given cards to five more people, who would they have been? Now think of five people who are not your enemies, but who nevertheless you would not consider giving cards to. Using the data you have generated for yourself, come up with a principle that can explain your choice about who and who not to give birthday cards to. Make your own independent assessment about the degree to which your explanation corresponds with the main tenets of exchange theory.

Part IV

Taking Stock of Sociological Theory: A Recap

This book is not encyclopedic. Material covered has been trimmed to a bare minimum and explained in a clear fashion. Anyone who might be tested on sociological theory or the history of the discipline really should know everything covered in this book. Nevertheless, the various details are never as important as the recurrent themes.

There are five recurrent themes of this book. First, it means something particular when we say sociology is a science. It means (a) we want to improve our descriptions of the interpersonal attachments, shared beliefs, and systemic interconnections and constraints; (b) we want to be able to explain variation, either differences between cases or change within a single case over time; (c) we want to understand the consequences of different patterns of attachments, shared beliefs, and systemic interconnections and constraints; (d) we want to be honest and explicit about the axiomatic assumptions we are making when we try to model sociological processes; (e) we want to be as accurate as possible in articulating our best current approximation of explanatory principles that can allow us to understand and make predictions about variability in outcomes in the social world; (f) we want to subject our provisional principles to repeated testing under different circumstances in order to define limiting conditions and otherwise refine our axioms and improve our principles; and (g) we aim for theoretical understanding revealing enough to help guide us as we work for better organizational, community, and societal outcomes.

Second, sociology is a coherent discipline with a coherent history. It is fundamentally understandable in its rough outline. Durkheim, Weber, Marx, and Mead raised questions that make fundamental sense for sociologists to investigate, and successive generations of sociologists have pressed forward with those questions.

The third theme of the book is that the various theoretical perspectives that have developed in our discipline are not mutually exclusive. While each of the perspectives has a different focus, all have fundamental points of synergy. This means they help us to understand different pieces of the same broad tapestry. Sociological awareness is incomplete when it disregards any of the perspectives covered in this book. Richer, deeper, fuller understanding with more immediate application comes from drawing from multiple perspectives. Privileging a single perspective to the exclusion of all the others is equivalent to wearing blinders.

Fourth, sociologists know something. In fact we know a lot. And much of what we know can be communicated in a few useful axioms and a few very robust explanatory principles. These axioms and principles can no doubt be reworked and improved on. But for now, the wording used in this book serves as a reasonable first approximation for some important sociological insights, so readers will not walk away from this book empty-handed. Those axioms and principles can serve as an analytical tool kit.

The fifth and final theme of this book is that sociological theory is intellectually alive. We deal with key questions that cry out for treatment. Sociology is a vibrant discipline arriving at useful insights about important topics.

Part IV of the book begins with a brief summary highlighting the first, second, and third issues listed above. This summary is followed by a short postscript reviewing a few pivotal questions facing sociological theorists as we move forward from this point in time. The postscript is followed by a compendium of the axioms presented in this book and then a compendium of the principles presented in this book. These axioms and principles are useful tools for anyone who must negotiate sociological terrain. In other words, these are useful tools for everyone. The book concludes with answer sheets for the chapter review tests.

SOCIOLOGY AS A COHERENT DISCIPLINE RATHER THAN AN INCOHERENT DISCIPLINE

Keeping the Whole Forest in View

Aside from learning a lot of specific details and amassing a useful analytical tool kit, there are three general lessons the reader should take from this book. First, theory is both the beginning and the end of the scientific process. Second, despite the fact that the discipline of sociology is broad and expansive, it is nevertheless a coherent field. Readers of this book should have acquired an integrated overview of the discipline, which is something every sociologically trained person should have. Third, when considered together, sociology's various theoretical perspectives offer a richer framework for analysis than does any of the perspectives taken in isolation.

THEORY IN SCIENCE

Theory gains its scientific significance from intimate connection with research. The scientific method begins with theory. It starts with conceptualization allowing for formulation of a research question. This is followed by identifying axioms that help us model what may be happening and the articulation of explanatory principles to be tested. The data collection aspects of science that people normally think of when they hear the word "research" really only begin when a theoretically grounded and purposeful test has been designed. Unless a research protocol is theoretically well grounded and purposeful, its "science" value is compromised. Good science begins with theory. And the less mature the science, the more crucial it is that practitioners really understand the rightful connection between theory and research in science, in order to prevent the process from driving for years down a dead end.

Just as important as its beginning in theory, the scientific method also ends with theory. Whenever research activity begins to reach a conclusion, the scientific method involves revisiting our body of theory for the purpose of trying to learn lessons that translate into more mature and powerful theoretical understanding. The ultimate objective is to revisit the axioms and principles we started with and either add to or modify them, or learn something useful about the way they operate and the conditions under which they apply. Once all this is understood, it should leave readers with the realization that sociology is a science and that sociologists are practitioners of a science. We are in the business of explaining how cases change over time and how differences emerge between cases.

Science is defined by a culture of evidence. Evidence is not just data. Data become evidence when they are marshaled in ways that help us challenge and stretch our understandings. Data become evidence when they are used in a meaningful test.

A CONCISE UNDERSTANDING OF THE
HISTORY OF THE DISCIPLINE

Everyone studying a subject should have an understanding of the basic outline of that discipline's history. Readers of this book should now understand the basic outline of sociology's history, and should be able to speak and write intelligibly about the evolution of sociology as a discipline.

The nineteenth century was a time of convulsive change. Both Western Europe and the United States were overwhelmingly rural and agricultural in 1801 and were substantially urbanizing and industrializing at a rapid pace by 1899. Governments were autocratic or just beginning to be meaningfully democratic in 1801, and they were under substantial pressure to democratize or make the promise of democracy more meaningful by 1899. Throughout the nineteenth century, democratization was viewed with suspicion by vested interests everywhere, because at the end of the eighteenth century democratization had been accompanied by bloody revolution in France and a war for independence in what was to become the United States of America.

At the same time, the scientific revolution offered hope for a better life. The natural and biological sciences had improved transportation, magnified productive capacity, and begun to combat disease. This gave cause for optimism, and many people began to imagine that it would be possible to develop social sciences to inform better public policy and more effective public programs. The social sciences, it was hoped, could yield the insight necessary to build better societies—more peaceful and more prosperous societies that would allow greater freedom of opportunity for personal growth and improvement. Brazil (the most recent country to elect a sociologist as president) actually emblazoned a motto of the scientific age on its flag.

In that environment, a few dozen people working on the borders of other disciplines outlined the parameters of what was to become sociology. Some of the most important of these were Emile Durkheim and W. I. Thomas working on the borders anthropology, George Herbert Mead and Charles Horton Cooley working on the borders of psychology, and Max Weber, Karl Marx, Vilfredo Pareto, and Thorstein Veblen working on the borders of economics. They generated a pool of insights that were to become the intellectual foundation stones for all the sociological work to follow. They focused our attention on the importance of community transition and organization/disorganization. They alerted us to the importance of definition of situation and self-concept. They understood that people organized their lives around roles that were in some sense shaped by values. And they recognized that economic life, around which human activity often revolved, could be most adequately understood within the context of an encompassing sociological framework.

Besides fixing the parameters of the new discipline, with its focus on social attachments (direct ties, and also institutional connections, often involving regulatory controls) and shared beliefs, the earliest pioneers in sociology gave us an epistemology of science. This is most evident with Durkheim, who used the language of science and showed us how scientific method could be followed in sociology as long as we kept our focus on social facts, that is, characteristics true of groups or collective units and not simply of individuals. But it was also true of people such as Marx who were less comfortable with the language of science. Marx, whose contribution to economics is of arguable significance, made a stunningly important set of sociological discoveries by identifying conditions leading to group polarization and conflict. Intergroup antagonism is most likely to develop when there are big differences between groups, a lot of competition for scarce resources, and few avenues for mobility, and when opposing groups are internally homogeneous, have a lot of internal communication, and are characterized by high levels of symbolic unification.

Then came intellectual giants of a different sort, the great synthesizers such as Talcott Parsons and, to a somewhat lesser extent, George Homans. Talcott Parsons became the standard bearer for structural–functionalism when he synthesized insights from Durkheim, Weber, and Pareto to show us how long-term societal trends, such as democratization and the spread of universal education, could be understood as structural responses to meet societal needs. And George Homans became the first standard bearer for exchange theory when he translated the basic principles of behavioral psychology and utilitarian economics into a formation that could be easily applied to the daily "commerce" of social life.

By the mid-twentieth century, as different theoretical paradigms began to form and there were many more sociologists to apply them, there was an explosion of work that bore fruit. A small sample includes studies of core self-concept, role strain, reference groups, equilibrium processes within organizations, and the changing contours of class and class conflict in contemporary society. All of these added to our understanding of the questions that have remained integral to sociological investigation since the time of the discipline's founders.

Finishing this book, readers should have a "whole forest" overview of the history of sociology. When we hear of a person or perspective whose name we recognize, we should have a general sense for where that person or perspective fits on an evolutionary tree of sociological ideas.

MUTUAL COMPATIBILITY OF PERSPECTIVES

Sociology students often leave their first sociology classes feeling that sociological theory is a combat zone in which one perspective should be victorious and all others should be vanquished. This is wrong. This would be an intellectually wasteful, a self-limiting, and a stifling view of the discipline. Theory is insight, and insight is a terrible thing to waste. And that's what you do when you dismiss a perspective before discovering how it can be used.

Ninety years ago, natural scientists did not ask whether the theory of electricity was to be preferred over the theory of magnetism or vice versa. They asked what we had to know to link those then distinct theoretical frameworks for understanding different parts of our observable reality into a more integrated, consistent, informative understanding of the physical universe (electromagnetism).

Likewise, sociological theory is most informative when we take advantage of the richness of all our perspectives rather than privileging one by discounting the others. The key is to understand how those different understandings actually do link up at synergy points, so that they mutually inform each other.

Although the mid-twentieth century was characterized by a certain degree of insularity, with people who were interested in developing one theoretical perspective tending to ignore or discount the others, any antipathy between perspectives became progressively counterproductive, and quite thankfully it has worn away with time. Conditions are now right to make significant theoretical progress.

What is the current of sociology with regard to its explanatory frameworks? Sociologists uniformly embrace the view that we cannot understand the real world shaping our lives without taking into account class and stratification (the focus of conflict theory) and values and organizational and institutional patterns (the focus of structural–functionalism). Nor can we understand society without recognizing that people do sometimes have agency (a focus of symbolic interactionism). Nor can we understand the role of agency without considering goal-maximizing behavior (a focus of exchange theory) or our ability to reconsider interpretations and adjust behavior (another focus of symbolic interactionism). Universal acceptance of these simple points makes sociology a multiple paradigm discipline in which each paradigm brings value.

And whatever insights we do feel we are able to articulate, we must always be open to the possibility that we are wrong (the fundamental tenet of science). The postmodernist admonition that we always need to ask ourselves what interests current beliefs support is a kind of healthy skepticism science should never sacrifice.

CONCLUSION

As promised from the beginning, this book is anything but encyclopedic. The purpose is to introduce theory in a way that relays a good general understanding and presents an accurate overview. This book is not meant as an ending ("yeah, the last theory I will ever have to read") but rather as a beginning ("here is something I can use; I want to look more deeply into some of these theorists and theories"). If the author has been successful, readers will feel comfortable discussing theory in general, applying ideas covered in the text to the real world, and going on to read more sociological theory. Sociology and sociological theory are relevant and useful! Recalling the lessons within these pages should help to keep the whole forest in view.

Postscript

Central to the vitality of sociology as a science, people entering the field need to be open to the possibility of fruitful knowledge growth through theoretically grounded inquiry. This book is not alone in pressing that claim. But in comparison with other theory books, this one more clearly and consistently makes the case that theory should be understood with reference to role in the research process.

What should our research questions be? One of the great things about sociology is that it is broad and extensive. Certain questions generate special interest because they relate to areas of possible linkage points between sociology's main explanatory frameworks. Some illustrations follow. All these questions are likely to be important in the future. They help define the present state and future promise of sociology as an explanatory science.

Structural–Functionalism and Conflict: When and how do special interests hijack the corridors of public power, and when and how is that hijacking blocked or moderated?

Structural–Functionalism, Conflict, and Exchange: When and how are costs externalized?

Structural–Functionalism, Conflict, and Symbolic Interactionism: When and how do feedback mechanisms generate full and accurate assessment, and when and how do feedback mechanisms produce skewed and inaccurate assessment?

Iowa versus Chicago: When and how is the "core self" energized, and when and how is it held in check?

Chicago versus Structural–Functionalism: When and how do primary and/or reference groups transmit and reaffirm societal messages, and when do they mute, transform, or displace societal messages with locally constructed messages?

Exchange and Symbolic Interactionism: What comes to be most valued? How? Why?

Invitation to Further Dialogue

Science begins and ends with theory, and science is a team sport. I am open to collegial exchange with anyone who would like to press forward into the domain of sociological theory. A lot needs to be done, and diversity of talent and experience is needed if we are to make theoretical progress as fast as we might.

Charles Powers, cpowers@scu.edu
Sociology Program
Department of Anthropology and Sociology
Santa Clara University
Santa Clara, California 95053–0261

COMPENDIUM OF AXIOMS

Twelve Commonly Made Assumptions Helping Us to Make Predictions

CHAPTER 2

Definition of Situation Axiom: *People respond to situations according to what they believe to be true about the situation, rather than what is actually true.*

Rational Choice Axiom: *People tend to make benefit-maximizing decisions based on their priorities.*

CHAPTER 4

Founder Effects Axiom: *Those interests and concerns of founding figures that become active parts of institutional memory tend to shape the activities of others for a long time to come.*

CHAPTER 8

Values Axiom: *As a system of values becomes more deeply embedded and more uniformly held by people in a society, then institutional forms and relational patterns are progressively modified in ways that maximize adherence to core values.*

CHAPTER 9

Self/Identity Axiom: *The individual traits people think of themselves as having, and the memberships that people regard as salient, reflect how people have responded to us in the past and seem to define how others think we are.*

CHAPTER 10

Cultural Adaptation Axiom: *Migrants change a great deal during migration, and they are highly selective in the aspects of culture they retain and highly innovative in how they modify those aspects of culture to meet new needs.*

CHAPTER 11

Form Follows Function Axiom: *Form follows function in the sense that widespread patterns of structural change emerge as systemic responses to meet new needs or correct for poor performance in the face of old needs.*

CHAPTER 12

Structure Inequality Axiom: *The social structural arrangements that evolve and survive tend to be those that protect the interests of more powerful people at the expense of less powerful people.*

Corruption of Power Axiom: *The powerful do not loosen the grip of exploitation without being pressed to.*

CHAPTER 13

Social Location Axiom: *People tend to think that what they have personally encountered or heard from the people closest to them is authentic and representative and generally true of the way the world is.*

CHAPTER 14

Symbolic Exchange Axiom: *Nonutilitarian signs of recognition and acceptance are the principal ways through which social ties are revived and affirmed.*

Power Imbalance Axiom: *Social settings tend to change in the direction of greater symmetry of power and dependence, or toward development of formal and informal limits on exploitation in nonsymmetric relationships.*

COMPENDIUM OF PRINCIPLES

Eighteen Testable Laws for Sociology

CHAPTER 2

Rational Action Principle: *Other things being equal, the higher the value assigned to a goal, the lower the expected cost of a plan to achieve that goal, the greater the probability of success of the plan, and the less attractive are projected cost/benefit ratios of possible alternative courses of action in pursuit of this or other goals, then the more likely a person is to implement the plan under consideration.*

Anger Principle: *Other things being equal, anger increases in magnitude as a function of the degree to which actual outcomes fall short of expected outcomes.*

CHAPTER 3

Conflict/Cohesion Principle: *Other things being equal, cohesion within groups increases as a function of the degree of conflict between groups.*

CHAPTER 5

Principle of Social Control: *Other things being equal, the more integrated the members of a group or community are (the more interconnected they are and the more bound they are to a common set of beliefs) and the fewer offsetting ties people have to other groups or communities, then the greater the level of social control the group or community will exert over its members.*

CHAPTER 6

Principle of Evolution: *Other things being equal, the smaller subpopulations are and the less contact they have with each other, the more rapidly and more dramatically they will differentiate from each other.*

Principle of Supply and Demand: *Other things being equal, the more scarce something is, and the more sought after it is, then the more costly it becomes, the more incentive potential producers have to enter into production of it, and the more incentive consumers have to look for substitutes for it.*

Uncertainty Principle of Hierarchy: *Other things being equal, the greater the risk of uncertainty implicit in market solutions, the more cost-effective market solutions need to be in order to make them rational in comparison with hierarchy as a mode of organization.*

Innovation/Complexity Principle of Networking: *Other things being equal, the advisability of network/strategic alliance solutions to organizational challenges is a positive function of the complexity of activity and the necessity to maintain ongoing creativity and innovation in order to remain competitive.*

CHAPTER 7

Principle of Intergroup Antagonism: *Other things being equal, the greater the level of inequality between groups, the greater the homogeneity within groups, the more substantial the barriers to mobility between groups, and the greater the level of intergroup competition over scarce resources, then the more likely members of both groups are to have a sense of distinct identity and the more profound intergroup antagonisms will be.*

CHAPTER 9

Principle of Role Redefinition: *Other things being equal, people have the greatest latitude for customizing role relationships when (a) symbolic interaction is most frequent, longest lasting, and emotionally most intense; (b) people enjoy autonomy and perform their roles without much direct observation by others; (c) anticipatory socialization and validation for conventional performance are relatively weak; (d) peer group support of customization is clear; and (e) everyone involved in the relationship wants to redefine roles in the same direction.*

CHAPTER 11

The Principle of Systemic Coupling: *Other things being equal, the more tightly coupled units are (the more communication between units, the more resource interdependence, the more meaningful the connection in a chain of command, the stronger the sense of common fate, and the higher the commitment to common values) and the more clearly defined common objectives are, then the less likely common objectives are to be supplanted by provincial ones and the more effective the pursuit of shared objectives will be.*

Principle of Structural Strain: *Other things being equal, the greater the awareness of disparity between values and common patterns of behavior, the more likely patterns of behavior are to change in the direction of greater consistency with core social values.*

CHAPTER 12

Pluralist Governance Principle: *Other things being equal, the more diverse economic activity and organized social life are, the more broadly distributed control over economic activity and organized social life is, the higher the level and broader the distribution of education and other forms of human capital, and the more diverse and open are channels of public communication, then the greater the number and broader the diversity of interest groups that will have the ability to influence the agendas of civic, government, and community organizations and the more pluralistic governance will be.*

Principle of Legitimate Authority: *Other things being equal, authority tends to be perceived as legitimate to the degree that (a) protection of rights and provision of services are thought to be reliable, (b) adjudication of grievances by administrative agents is seen as fair, and (c) ideology and information are skillfully used to deflect blame in the direction of internal opposition or external enemies.*

Principle of Intergroup Conflict: *Other things being equal, (a) the more pronounced intergroup antagonism becomes, (b) the more historical/symbolic unity there is within each group and the more historical/symbolic division there is between groups, and (c) the more communication there is within groups and the less communication there is between groups, then the more likely intergroup antagonism is to lead to organized conflict.*

Principle of Violent Conflict: *Other things being equal, the more recurrent and procedurally regulated conflict is, the less likely it is to turn violent.*

CHAPTER 13

Principle of Socialization: *Other things being equal, socialization is likely to be most effective to the degree that the person being socialized (a) depends on the socializing agent, (b) trusts the socializing agent, and (c) has an opportunity to act out or practice new norms and roles with peers.*

CHAPTER 14

Principle of Regulation: *Other things being equal, the extension of regulatory control over new spheres of activity by a branch of government is a positive function of (a) the magnitude of externalized costs that are* *understood to result from unregulated activity, (b) the degree to which a regulatory vacuum compromises the government's claim that it protects people, and (c) the legitimacy of the regulatory extension, and it is a negative function of (d) the degree to which the government is already overburdened with other concerns and commitments.*

Quiz Answers

CHAPTER 1

1. science
2. d
3. b
4. (a) micro, (b) meso, (c) macro
5. a
6. c

CHAPTER 2

1. a
2. d
3. d
4. b
5. b

CHAPTER 3

1. Focus on differences or change to be explained; advance a principle that might explain that difference or change; identify one or more research hypotheses that could be used to test the principle; test the research hypotheses using real-world information; use results in order to rethink and improve upon the original theoretical explanation.

2. Simmel's Conflict/Cohesion Principle: *Other things being equal, cohesion within groups increases as a function of the degree of conflict between groups.*
3. b
4. c
5. b
6. b
7. c

CHAPTER 4

1. a reign of terror similar to that experienced during the French Revolution
2. b
3. a

CHAPTER 5

1. Auguste Comte
2. Harriet Martineau
3. Emile Durkheim
4. Symbols help us distinguish who is in a group or category from those who are not, and they remind people what kinds of behavior membership in a group or category is supposed to translate into.
5. Principle of Social Control: *Other things being equal, the more integrated the members of a group or community are (the more interconnected they are and the more bound they are to a common set of beliefs) and the fewer offsetting ties people have to other groups or communities, then the greater the level of social control the group or community will exert over its members.*

CHAPTER 6

1. The characteristics of a perfect market are (1) people must be engaged in exchange that we can at least loosely conceptualize as having "buyers" and "sellers"; (2) there must be freedom of choice, so that each buyer and each seller can decide if the terms of exchange are acceptable; (3) there must be many potential exchange partners, so that free-

dom of choice is real; and (4) "barriers" to entry and exit have to be minimal.

2. Principle of Evolution: *Other things being equal, the smaller subpopulations are and the less contact they have with each other, the more rapidly and more dramatically they will differentiate from each other. Globalization reduces cultural heterogeneity.*

3. Uncertainty Principle of Hierarchy: *Other things being equal, the greater the risk of uncertainty implicit in market solutions, the more cost-effective market solutions need to be in order to make them rational in comparison with hierarchy as a mode of organization. Thus, uncertainty raises the value of hierarchical organizing strategies.*

CHAPTER 7

1. Marx's Principle of Intergroup Antagonism: *Other things being equal, the greater the level of inequality between groups, the greater the homogeneity within groups, the more substantial the barriers to mobility between groups, and the greater the level of intergroup competition over scarce resources, then the more likely members of both groups are to have a sense of distinct identity and the more profound intergroup antagonisms will be.*

2. Dialectical explanations suggest that events inexorably lead toward dramatic change in the fundamental character of the society. Marx was a dialectical theorist because he believed that one economic system gives way to another system governed by an altogether different set of rules. For example, capitalism grew out of the ruins of feudalism. Cyclical theories focus on rhythmic changes such as the business cycle, suggesting that relatively bad times create conditions for good times to follow, and vice versa. The business cycle is an example. The basic nature of the system remains relatively unchanged, even as cycles move through their peaks and troughs.

3. For Marx, class is defined in terms of social relationship to means of production, for example, whether one lives by selling his or her own labor or by buying and directing the labor of others.

CHAPTER 8

1. b
2. traditional, charismatic, and rational–legal

3. hierarchical chain of command, functional division of labor, hiring based on training rather than nepotism, decisions made according to a system of codified and uniformly applied rules, and records as property of office rather than office holders.

4. Weber's Values Axiom: *As a system of values becomes more deeply embedded and more uniformly held by people in a society, then institutional forms and relational patterns are progressively modified in ways that maximize adherence to core values.*

CHAPTER 9

1. "How do people manage to adjust to one another effectively?"
2. Dewey—Pragmatism; Charles Horton Cooley—looking-glass self
3. Self-concept is our sense of our own qualities as individual people. Identity refers to group memberships that are inescapably important, usually because they matter so much to others that they dictate how the world responds to us.
4. The process of symbolic interaction people work through as they adjust to others involves:
   a. reading gestures
   b. role taking
   c. taking stock of the self
   d. imaginative rehearsal
   e. adjusted response

CHAPTER 10

1.
   a. 3
   b. 4
   c. 2
   d. 1
2. The tipping point seems to occur when the members from one community moving into the territory of another reach about 30 percent of the population in the new area.

3. The Cultural Adaptation Axiom tells us to expect people who speak like ethnic traditionalists to actually be creative innovaters.

CHAPTER 11

1. Structure changes when functional problems magnify. And the structural forms that evolve help meet system needs.
2. Evolutionary patterns of structural change:

role upgrading
structural differentiation
inclusion
value generalization

3. Robert K. Merton (a) introduced the Harvard Pareto circle to the works of Durkheim and (b) emphasized the importance of distinguishing between manifest functions (obvious and intended outcomes) and latent functions (unintended or intended consequences).

CHAPTER 12

1. Pronounced intergroup antagonism, historical/symbolic unity within groups and historical/symbolic division between groups, and good communication within groups and poor communication between groups (see the Principle of Intergroup Conflict).
2. When the level of concentration of economic control and human capital is greatest (see the Pluralism Principle).
3. three

CHAPTER 13

1. Chicago and Iowa are both about coconstructed change. Impression management and altercasting, on which dramaturgical analysis focuses, are both about a relatively static and fictional image that is projected from a single source rather than cocrafted.
2. Symbolic interactionists of the Iowa school believe that outcomes in social situations are rather predictable because the core self-concepts

of people in a situation incline them to interpret and react in particular ways, and this channels outcomes in a certain direction.

3. a. "Identity" refers to group memberships that are inescapably important, usually because they matter so much to others that they dictate how the world responds to us.

   b. "Roles" are rights and obligations normally expected of anyone in that particular social position.

CHAPTER 14

1. True
2. True

Index

About the Author

Charles H. Powers is professor of sociology at Santa Clara University, where he has taught since 1986. His former full-time teaching positions were at Talladega College and at Indiana University. In addition to sociology, Professor Powers has taught business administration and gerontology, and has lectured for executive development programs and the U.S. Chambers of Commerce. His other book publications are *Vilfredo Pareto* (author), *The Transformation of Democracy* (editor), *Post-Industrial Lives* (coauthor), and *The Emergence of Sociological Theory* (coauthor). Professor Powers has a special interest in the study of role change and in the analysis of organizational cultures that foster innovation. His writings broadly address the integration of economics and sociology.